History of the Income Tax

By

Adam Starchild

International Law & Taxation Publishers
London

History of the Income Tax

by
Adam Starchild

ISBN: 1-893713-41-5

International Law & Taxation Publishers
London
http://www.internationallawandtaxationpublishers.com

Contents

A Brief Look at Taxes through History 1

America before the Income Tax: Where Did the
    Government's Money Come From? 9

    Taxes in the Early United States 11
    The Civil War and Income Tax 14
    The Revenue Act of 1917 25
    The Making of Tax Policy 27
    The Battle over Taxable Income 30
    The Call for a Progressive Tax 36
    The Case for Exemptions 40
    Personal and Corporate Income Taxes 42

The Evolving Federal Income Tax 45

    The Great Rate Debate 46
    Creation of the Modern Income Tax 49
    Taxes in the 1980s and 1990s 52
    The Modern Driving Forces of the Federal Income
        Tax 55
    Do the Rich Really Pay Their Fair Share? 57

Tax Havens of the West 61

    Antigua and Barbuda 62
        Investment and Taxes 62
    Anguilla 64
        Economy and Taxes 65
    Barbados 66
        Economy and Taxes 67

The Bahamas **72**
    Economy and Taxes 73
Bermuda **75**
    Economy and Taxes 76
Cayman Islands **78**
    Economy and Taxes 79
Ecuador **81**
    Economy and Taxes 82
Guatemala **85**
    Economy and Taxes 85
Honduras **89**
    Economy and Taxes 90
The Republic of Ireland **94**
    Economy and Taxes 95
Madeira **100**
    Economy and Taxes 101
Malta **108**
    Economy and Taxes 109
Monaco **111**
    Economy and Taxes 112
Panama **113**
    Economy and Taxes 115
Portugal **117**
    Economy and Taxes 118
Puerto Rico **121**
    Economy and Taxes 122
St. Kitts and Nevis **128**
    Economy and Taxes 129
Turks and Caicos **133**
    Economy and Taxes 134
The United Kingdom **135**
    Economy and Taxes 136

The Republic of Ireland 139
    Economy and Taxes 140
Tax Havens of the East 147
Dubai 147
    Economy and Taxes 148
Guam 150
    Economy and Taxes 151
Hong Kong 153
    Economy and Taxes 155
Jordan 158
    Economy and Taxes 160
The Commonwealth of the Northern Mariana
    Islands 162
    Economy and Taxes 164
Republic of the Philippines 166
    Economy and Taxes 167
Seychelles 170
    Economy and Taxes 170
The Republic of Singapore 174
    Economy and Taxes 175
About the Author 179

A Brief Look at Taxes through History

Taxes are a compulsory contribution individuals and/or businesses must make to the government. The primary purpose of a tax is to fund governmental activity, however, the purposes of governmental activities may be broadly defined. Along with funding the necessities of government, the purpose of taxation frequently expands to include economic and social objectives. Taxes may be used as a method for developing a strong, vibrant economy by fostering or limiting certain businesses, or they may be used as a means of redistributing wealth and encouraging social reform.

Taxes have been a part of society from the time the first governments developed. Payment of animal skins to a chief, who could use the animal skins to buy weapons which he would use to supply warriors who would defend the village, was a type of primitive tax. Taxes have been used by governments to pay for public works, fund wars, control economies through tariffs on imports and exports, and, sadly, fill the coffers of rulers at the expense of the ruled.

1

Some of the oldest records of civilization tell of taxes. The following examples are by no means complete but indicate how long taxes have been a part of people's economic lives:

- 2000 BC, clay records discovered in Iraq tell of onerous taxes.

- 1400 BC, Egyptian records detail subjects paying taxes to their Pharaoh.

- 600 BC, the first graduated income tax was in use in Greece.

- 300 BC, the Ptolemy dynasty of Egypt instituted various taxes, including tariffs on imports, poll taxes on salt, legal documents, sales and rental of goods, fees for grazing cattle on state land, and a tax on produce.

- 125 BC, tax collection in the Roman Empire is a well established system.

- 1050 AD, the story of Lady Godiva highlights a tax protest in England.

- 1427, income and property taxes are instituted in in Florence, Italy.

- 1450, in Mexico taxes could be paid to the Aztec government in the form of exotic feathers.

- 1643, a faculty tax is adopted in New Plymouth, Massachusetts. A precursor of income taxes, a faculty tax was applied to a person's "faculties," his or her ability to earn income from property, trade, or a skill. In time most of the colonies were to establish faculty taxes.

- 1793, the first general income tax is established in France.

Taxes come in many forms. Throughout much of history taxes were seldom paid in money but rather in the form of produce, commodities, or labor. In the Middle Ages because society was not advanced economically, rulers who needed troops for protecting their holdings, or workers to build bridges, roads, or other public works, were happy to accept payments in the form of grain, livestock, or a commitment of work or military service from their subjects. The economics were simple. Once a workforce was organized, they would need food to eat, and thus some landowners would be required to provide grain or livestock. This basic system underlies the modern tax structures of today. The government collects taxes in the form of money, and the money in theory is spent on the functions of government.

Governments have been known to be innovative in devising ways to tax their subjects. During the time of Pericles, ancient Athens established an assortment of taxes, including: import and export tariffs, a sales tax, traffic tolls, harbor fees, license fees, and property taxes. Note that while not all of the above have "tax" in their name, each, unquestionably, is a tax. Taxes have many names.

Following is a list of common taxes:

- income tax – a tax calculated on income.

- property tax – a tax calculated on the assessed value of property a taxpayer owns. Property taxes are among the oldest taxes, dating to ancient times.

- import and export duties – taxes assessed on the value of specific products, goods, or services brought into or sent out of a country.

- excise taxes – taxes, sometimes called fees, on specific commodities or services. Excise taxes are are placed cigarettes and liquor, as well as many luxury items.

- sales taxes – taxes calculated on sales transactions. Sales taxes are especially popular on retail items and are common state taxes.

- inheritance taxes – taxes alculated on the assets passed from the deceased to his or her heirs.

- value-added tax – taxes based on what people own, buy, or transfer. Although they are relatively new in taxation, value-added taxes are common in many countries. Some tax experts believe that a value-added tax is in time likely for the United States.

The above are the basic taxes. There are others. Licensing fees, for example, may not in a technical sense be called a tax, however, their purpose is the same: they pay for the cost of government. In the past poll taxes were popular in many places. A poll, or head, tax was a tax placed on an individual, whether he was a free man or a slave. Harbor fees and traffic tolls are yet other types of taxes that most people do not usually think of as being taxes, but in fact they are.

Even religions enjoy a form of taxation. In the Christian and Jewish faiths the tradition of tithing is little more than taxation. Followers of the faith are expected to pay the first tenth of their earnings to their churches or synogogues.

Taxes were an important part of economic life in the ancient and medieval worlds. So well established were taxes in the ancient world that the Bible describes tax collectors as being despised by the people. Indeed, many governments employed legions of scribes to record the property and taxable possessions and transactions of their people. After conquering England in 1066, William the Conqueror ordered compilation of the *Domesday Book*. While at first many thought the registry was merely an attempt at counting the people of his domain, a type of early census, it soon became clear that the purpose of the book was to make accurate tax accounting a certainty. William needed money to pay for his conquest, and what better way than through taxes?

Throughout history taxes have been levied on property, income, occupation, and status. Taxes were paid in livestock, farm produce, military service, or labor, but no matter the method of payment, people have resented paying taxes. While it is true that a government requires funds to function and carry out its mission, the lesson history teaches is that most governments levy far more taxes than they require. It is vital, therefore, for citizens to hold their leaders accountable for instituting equitable tax codes.

A historical review of tax systems clearly shows that effective systems share specific elements. Most tax experts would agree on the following:

- Fairness. A tax code must be fair. Those paying the tax should be taxed in a manner and amount based on their ability to pay. Simply put, people of greater means should pay more taxes than people of lesser means. However, fairness also addresses the issue of burden. No one should be assessed taxes that are burdensome. Furthermore, taxes should be limited in every way possible.

Only the essential needs of government should be supported through taxation.

- Clarity. Tax laws should be clear and unambiguous. Whenever there is a lack of clarity in the tax code, people lose confidence in the system. Moreover, complex, indecipherable tax codes open the way for abuse on the part of the government and cheating on the parts of taxpayers.

- Efficiency. A tax system should be efficient in the manner it collects and distributes money. A tax system that is inefficient wastes resources and inspires resentment.

In their efforts to achieve overall fairness in their tax codes, most nations resort to various taxes. While income taxes and property taxes account for much of the tax revenues throughout the modern world, excise taxes, special business taxes (usually under the guise of fees, licenses, etc.), and social security taxes are other common sources of revenue, which diversify a nation's tax code.

The concept of taxes likely goes back to the most primitive of human societies in which members of the tribe bestowed upon their leader items of value to ensure his protection. From this simple form of tribute elaborate systems of taxation eventually arose.

America before the Income Tax: Where Did the Government's Money Come From?

According to Ben Franklin, "...In this world, nothing can be said to be certain, except death and taxes." Those words, attributed to Franklin in 1789, remain true today and likely will always be true. In Franklin's day, no tax code in the world contained an income tax. Given their historical opposition against taxes, and the fact that the Founding Fathers had included in the Constitution a provision severely restricting the implementation of a national tax, it would have seemed that U.S. citizens would have been spared any form of general income tax. Indeed, for many years, this proved to be true.

During the early days of colonization, the founders of a colony were expected to raise the capital for the colony's establishment. Some of these men had their own wealth from which to draw while others petitioned funds from family, friends, and supporters. Most of this money was spent on the basic needs of the colonists and little was given over to public projects. The colonists themselves were expected to build their new homes with their own capital and sweat.

As colonies grew and colonial governments developed beyond the stage of the town meeting hall, however, it became clear that government would have to be funded. Taxes became reality, but they still remained modest in scope and effect on wallets. Colonial governments derived most of the revenues from poll taxes, also known as head taxes, property taxes, and taxes on some products and services. Many of the colonies also eventually instituted faculty taxes, which were based on the property or "faculties" of people. These faculties could be interpreted as one's abilities, skills, or trades with which he could earn income. The greater one's faculties, the higher his tax. Introduced in 1643 in New Plymouth, Massachusetts, by the time of the American Revolution most of the colonies had some form of faculty tax. Because of its link to income (or the ability to earn income), some scholars consider faculty taxes to be an early form of income tax.

While such taxes were at most a minor irritation to colonists of the 1600 and early 1700s, by the mid 1700s taxes on things such as sugar, molasses, and tea, and of course, the hated stamp tax, infuriated enough people that taxes became a rallying cry of revolutionaries. When they study U.S. history, most American children learn about the phrase "No taxation without representation," which underscores the major tax complaint of the colonists: the British Parliament's unilateral decisions on colonial tax policy.

By the early 1770s, tax opposition in the colonies had grown to the point where many colonists simply ignored paying. Faced with such disregard of its laws, the British increased taxes and sent more troops to the colonies in an effort to put down resistance. Rather than quelling the protests, the actions only unified the colonists in their anti-tax cause. The Boston Tea Party, 1773, was as much an act of protest against the Tea Tax as it was an act of defiance against what many colonists felt to be British repression. The Declaration of Independence came three years later in 1776.

Taxes in the Early United States

In the years immediately following independence from Great Britain, the young United States did not have any form of national tax. Given the fact that taxation was one of the major causes of the Revolutionary War, it is not difficult to understand that the institution of new taxes did not rank high on the fledgling government's list of priorities. To have fought a war primarily about taxes only to devise new ones was hardly on anyone's mind. This policy, unfortunately, had its drawbacks.

To pay for its war of independence, the Continental Congress borrowed money from France, and, when this was not enough, simply printed its own. Without a strong, comprehensive tax system, the new government had little revenue and it did not take long for the government to default on its loans. When the government went bankrupt, it became obvious to most leaders that the national government required some powers of taxation. This was accomplished in the Constitution of 1789. Despite grumblings about states' rights, the consensus was that any national government, if it was to survive, needed some way to raise money to pay the nation's debts, maintain a common defense, and provide for the general welfare of the people of the United States.

The new country's first two presidents, George Washington and John Adams, moved quickly to raise revenues for the government through a rather broad system of taxation. During the years of these presidencies Congress enacted various excise taxes, including taxes on liquor, sugar, salt, and snuff. Taxes were also placed on homes, land, slaves, legal documents, auction sales, and bonds. If any of these taxes could be called excessive, it was the excise tax on whiskey, which led to the Whiskey Rebellion of 1794. With a gallon of whiskey costing 50 cents a gallon, a tax of 30 cents a gallon was enacted. This so angered farmers in Pennsylvania and other states who produced grain for distilling that they rebelled and Washington was forced to send militia to restore order.

With the inauguration of the country's third president, Thomas Jefferson, the tax wars fully returned. More concerned with the burdens taxes placed on citizens, Jefferson opposed most of the domestic taxes supported by Washington and Adams and worked successfully toward their appeal. By 1812, however, because of the new war with the British, many of the taxes Jefferson had repealed needed to be restored. Wars, without question, are costly.

Regardless of what their tax dollars may pay for, Americans have never liked taxes. For roughly the next forty years until the Civil War, taxes Americans paid directly to the government on their property and goods remained a small part of the government's overall revenues. Close to 90% of the government's revenues during these years were derived from tariffs, or taxes on imported goods.

The Civil War and Income Tax

Just like in the Revolutionary War, taxes again played a role in the Civil War. Much of the nation's manufacturing plants were located in the North. Because manufacturers wanted to protect their industries from lower-priced imports, the North wanted to keep tariffs on imports high. The power in the South resided in the hands of big plantation owners who wanted low tariffs. Because they were farmers and little industry existed in the South, they imported manufactured goods, and lower tariffs would make the goods and equipment they imported less expensive. While there were certainly several reasons that eventually ignited the war between the states, taxation was undoubtedly one of them.

The Civil War was enormously costly in terms of destruction, death, and money. It was also significant in terms of taxes, because the United States experienced its first income tax. In attempt to help cover the costs of the war, in July of 1862 Abraham Lincoln signed a sweeping new tax law that provided for both an income tax and inheritance tax. The income tax was modest with only a three percent tax on annual incomes between $600 and 10,000, and a five percent rate on higher incomes, however, the rates were soon increased to 10% on income over $5,000. Already one of the great potential faults of an income tax was revealed: once enacted, it is often a relatively simple matter to manipulate rates up or down. Even though less than one percent of the U.S. population was required to pay income tax during the Civil War – and the income tax paid for only a small percentage of the war's costs – it was not popular and in 1872 due to strong protest the tax was repealed.

Many hoped that the income tax controversy was concluded, but for some leaders of government, as well as private individuals who would have liked to see the role of government and its revenues expanded, the idea of an income tax became an important goal. Long after the Civil War the idea of an income tax continued to be debated. By the 1890s the debate had grown bitter with national leaders weighing in on both sides of the issue. Clearly there was a need for increased government revenues.

Throughout much of the 19th century, but especially during the last quarter, the United States experienced rapid industrialization. Society was being transformed from one based on agriculture to one of industry. As the new century approached, cities (and slums) were growing, new social classes emerged, new causes arose, and new political ideas came mainstream. It also became clear that the government could no longer rely mostly on tariffs for its revenue. It was a new

15

world, and demands escalated for new ways of running the country.

The Populist Movement, which traced its roots back to the Midwest of the 1870s where it championed the cause of farmers, had grown and gone national. By the early 1990s its adherrents included farmers and all manner of working people. One of the movement's core issues was adoption of an income tax.

It was not long before Democrats and Populists, who had gained control of Congress, spearheaded a coalition comprised of farmers, workers, and small-business owners in support of a national income tax. In 1894, Congress passed a law outlining a new income tax. With a rate of only 2% applied to personal income and corporate net income over $4,000, including inheritance and gifts, the new income tax affected few Americans. The few affected, however, were the well-to-do, who, led by Republicans supported by big business interests, challenged the new law and saw the Supreme Court reject it as unconstitutional in 1895.

The Court based its decision on what critics contend was a somewhat creative reading of the Constitution, which specified that any direct tax the federal government chose to enact had to be apportioned among states on the basis of population. Since the income tax was not apportioned in this manner, according to the Court it was unconstitutional. Many disagreed with the Court's ruling, and some in Congress wanted to quickly pass another income tax law but support had waned. Moreover, most legislators believed that the newly elected William McKinley would have vetoed an income tax bill anyhow.

With the defeat rendered by the Court, the argument over income tax subsided for a time. Within a few years after the turn of the century, however, Progressive Republican leaders mostly from the Midwest and West came to disagree with their party's leadership, mostly from the East, and now supported an income tax. The issue erupted once again.

By now the proponents of the income tax had much broad support. The Progressive Movement, heir to Populism and which had adherents across the nation, backed an income tax, most economists had come to believe that an income tax would serve the nation well, and evidence from those countries that had income taxes proved that the calamities opponents of the tax warned would come about did not. Income taxes appeared to be safe for an economy and surely could provide additional revenues for government.

Although William Howard Taft, the new Republican President, opposed income taxes, he also sensed possible defeat in Congress on the issue. To overcome the issue, Taft with other conservative Republican leaders concocted a strategy to propose a constitutional amendment allowing the government the power to enact an income tax. The idea was a simple one. Place the amendment before the states where it was unlikely a majority, 36, would ratify it. With an amendment thus defeated, coupled with the Supreme Court's rejection of an income tax in 1895, the issue of an income tax would be dead – at least in a legal sense.

Taft and his supporters miscalculated, however, and the amendment was ratified, with the 36th vote occurring in February of 1913. The 16th Amendment made an income tax a part of the U.S. Constitution. Taxes in the United States would never be the same.

Because an income tax is based on income, the questions of what income, how much, and in what way that income should be taxed become of paramount importance. Signing an income tax into law is one thing; ensuring that the income tax is fair for everyone is quite another. This was one of the major arguments of those not in favor of an income tax. Perhaps many of these people understood that once enacted, an income tax would be difficult if not impossible to legislate equitably.

As soon as the income tax law was enacted, interest groups quickly arose. The wealthy despised high rates, which they felt stifled economic growth, destroyed initiative, and undermined productivity. Advocates of the poor called for low rates, arguing that the poor should be allowed to keep what little money they had. In time members of the Middle Class felt that they suffered the greatest burdens of the income tax and they clamored for tax relief. The cries of excessive taxation led to exemptions for specific groups, which only worsened the problem for it convinced many people that the system was unfair. No matter what the rates on income are, most people consider them to be too high.

The income tax has clearly become one of the most contentious pieces of legislation in the nation's history. Because of the influence of powerful interests groups, the income tax has also become one of the most revised pieces of legislation in the history of the world. Politicians seem to be constantly tampering with the rates and adding and eliminating deductions and exemptions. While the sponsors of such actions claim the results will make the income tax more equitable, continuous revisions to the tax law only convince the typical taxpayer that the system is unfair and out of control.

Early Years of the Federal Income Tax

On October 3, 1913, the same day that the 16th Amendment was officially added to the Constitution, President Woodrow Wilson signed a bill enacting the federal income tax. Wilson had been elected in 1912 in part because of his support of an income tax and he was eager to sign it, not so much as an instrument with which to produce revenue for the federal government but as a means to achieve social fairness.

For years there had been a widening gulf between rich and poor in the United States. Because they tended to own companies and America had experienced a long period of industrial expansion throughout the latter part of the 19th century, the rich were growing enormously wealthier, while the poor, who labored long tedious hours in the businesses owned by the rich, were becoming poorer. One of the greatest burdens on the poor were tariffs and excise taxes. Although everyone had to pay them, such taxes consumed far more of the poor man's pay than the rich man's. In the minds of social reformers, an income tax would help to distribute the burden of taxes more equitably. Conceived in this manner, the income tax was a noble advancement in social policy.

Although the income tax was passed in October, 1913, it took effect on March 1, 1913. It applied to only 357,598 taxpayers, and the rates were modest: only 1% on taxable personal income above $3,000 for an individual and $4,000 for a married couple. Incomes above $20,000 were subject to additional rates, or a surtax, rising to 7% on incomes above $500,000. Such meager rates coupled with the fact that most Americans earned far less than $3,000 annually made the income tax of 1913 a low revenue producer. Indeed, of the federal government's overall revenues of $344.4 million in 1913, only 10% were derived from the income tax. Most of the government's revenues still came from tariffs and excise taxes.

This quickly changed with the coming of World War I. War in Europe severely affected the American economy. Exports to Europe fell, financial markets became unsteady, stocks plummeted in value, imports decreased, and industries cut back on production. Economic uncertainty prevailed. Because so much of its revenue depended on tariffs, government revenues fell from slightly over $73 million in July to $44.5 million in October. Although the economic news brightened somewhat in 1915 with European demand increasing for American goods to help in their war effort, overall government revenues remained down. Exports might have been rising, but imports, which accounted for tariff proceeds, were not. Moreover, President Wilson had been expanding the role of government by advancing major domestic programs and increasing administrative bodies to bring about reforms. Through the Underwood-Simmons tariff, he also lowered duties for the first time in 40 years, in part because he believed tariffs burdened the poor unfairly. At a time when he was decreasing the government's ability to raise revenue through tariffs, he also needed money to pay for his programs. Raising the rates of the income tax seemed to be the logical choice.

While Wilson was by no means an avid advocate of the income tax, he preferred tax increases to borrowing to pay for government expenditures, and he leaned toward increases in the income tax rather than increasing excise taxes and tariffs. Wilson, however, liked to keep above the arguments over taxation, preferring to focus his energies on governing, and he left the formulation and implementation of tax policy to the Congress.

With the Democrats in control of both houses, and consequently chairing all committees and subcommittees at a time when party loyalty was important, Wilson could leave tax matters to his party. The fact that strong proponents of the income tax chaired vital committees allowed Wilson to focus his energy on governing and not formulation of tax policy. One of these men was Claude Kitchen of North Carolina, the Chairman of the powerful House Ways and Means Committee, which spearheaded the income tax initiative in Congress. Kitchen also chaired the Democratic caucus, making him one of the most important men in the House. He was a strong believer in the House's role regarding revenue matters, and he also believed that tax laws should be written in a way that the rich bore the burden of payments. Another power broker of the House was Cordell Hull, of Tennessee, who chaired the Subcommittee on Internal Taxation. With strong Populist leanings, he, too, was a supporter of the income tax. Finally, John Sharp Williams of Mississippi, another Populist, led the Subcommittee on Income and Estate Taxes, and believed that the income tax could make the tax system fairer. In his view, the poor paid an unequal share of taxes because of custom duties.

With such leaders of Congress, who essentially shared the same views regarding the income tax, it is little wonder that Congress decided to raise more money through the income tax to avert a financial crisis. This could be done in various ways: raise rates, limit exemptions, increase the graduation of scales, and increase the surtax. In time, all of these done.

Income taxes soon comprised the bulk of federal revenues. By 1917, 2.7 million Americans were obligated to pay income taxes, up from the 357,598 of 1913, while the $35 million collected in income taxes in 1913 rose to $180.1 million. By 1918, 4.4 million Americans were obligated to pay income tax, and the number would only get higher. Legislators had learned the great power an income tax bestows, and by 1917 they were ready to use that power in full.

The Revenue Act of 1917

Although war had been raging in the trenches of Europe since 1914, the United States did not enter the war until 1917. To pay for the war, Congress passed the Revenue Act of 1917. The act was broad and far-reaching. It established twenty graduated rates for paying taxes on income, rising from 2%, which was levied on taxable income up to $2,000, up to 67% on all income over $2 million. The Act also reduced exemptions.

The result quickly became obvious: more Americans were paying more income tax than many proponents of the income tax had ever envisioned. The number of taxpayers had been rising from the establishment of the income tax, but now the tax base took a great leap forward. In 1918, revenues from the income tax surpassed all the revenue the government had collected from all sources in any other year before the income tax had been established. Responsible for such great revenues, the income tax became the foundation of the country's tax system.

People grumbled, the critics of the income tax quickly announced that this was one of their predictions, but because of the war effort, most criticism was somewhat muted. After all, individuals and corporations expected rates to fall once the war was won. They were disappointed; rates did not fall.

World War I proved to be far costlier than anyone would have imagined. From $1 million in 1916, the U.S. debt had rocketed to $25 billion by the war's end. To pay for the debt, Congress kept income tax rates high. Resentment over the tax grew. While the burden was still clearly being shouldered by the nation's more affluent citizens, it was becoming clear to many that the income tax placed enormous power in the hands of the government. When more revenue was required, legislators could simply increase tax rates. Fiscal responsibility and accountability were gone.

Cries increased for rate relief. Once the government became dependent upon the vast amounts of money the income tax could provide, however, significant tax relief was unlikely.

The Making of Tax Policy

The Constitution details that the power of formulating tax policy resides in the House of Representatives, which through the design of the Founding Fathers is the most representative branch of our government. While the greatest debates of the enactment and many subsequent revisions of the income tax occurred in the House, both Representatives and Senators aired their opinions and concerns over the pros and cons of an income tax. While presidents certainly have their opinions regarding tax policy, and they may attempt to convince members of Congress to support their views, the battles over the passage of an income tax were fought more among Congressmen than between Congress and the president. This was especially true in the years immediately following 1913.

Since its first appearance in political dialogue, the income tax has had both supporters and detractors. People around the country discussed the merit of an income tax and Congress was well aware of the concerns regarding the tax. By 1913, however, public opinion generally favored an income tax and this emboldened legislators to press ahead.

Passage of the income tax led to the rise of a new set of experts and policy makers. Prior to the income tax, federal revenues were derived primarily from tariffs and excise taxes, while property taxes were the foundation of state governments. Such taxation was rather straightforward with arguments focusing on what items were to be taxed and at what rate. With the arrival of a national income tax, however, a slew of questions arose and a host of experts emerged to answer them.

One of the most important questions the early income tax designers needed to answer was how much revenue the government would require from the income tax. Once that was answered, the tax base needed to be identified. Who, exactly, would be burdened with the bill? Would incomes below a certain level be exempt, and what would the tax rate be for incomes not exempt? Additionally, would the rates be progressive? If yes, how would they increase? Would there be a top limit? If yes, at what income?

Although the legislators supporting the income tax generally held strong views, they were not free from the concerns and questions of their constituents. Certainly these men relied upon the words and theories of economists who supported the income tax, but they also were aware of the opinions and worries of the public. At the time of the creation of the income tax, public opinion – particularly that of the masses who were most responsible for electing officials – weighed in on the side of the Progressives who favored a national tax as a method of equalizing the tax burden. The Democratic Congress was thus reasonably sure that its passing of an income tax would be accepted by the general public.

While the public may have cheered adoption of the income tax, most business owners and those of even modest wealth did not. They saw the income tax as a means of redistributing income, mostly theirs, and business associations throughout the country quickly formed tax groups to lobby Congress on behalf of the parent organization. Many of the country's largest businesses and corporations appointed individuals on their staff to advise the company on tax matters and keep abreast of the evolving tax laws. Today, most major businesses maintain entire tax departments for this purpose. Legislators soon felt the pressure from these groups.

Legislators also were influenced by various special interest groups, who believed their missions to be threatened by the income tax. Although such groups were rather small and poorly organized in the beginning, they have grown in strength and expertise and in some cases exert powerful influence over Congress. Consider the effect of today's conservative Christian groups, abortion foes, pro-choice groups, and advocates of the poor on legislators.

The Battle over Taxable Income

To most people the meaning of the word "income" seems obvious: money or equivalent items of value that are a result of one's labor, or, in the broader view, gains acquired through the growth of the value of investments. "Income" is not a simple concept to government tax planners, however. With income resulting from numerous potential sources – pay for labor, interest, growth of the value of stocks and bonds, the sale of real estate, inheritance, and gifts – the temptation to exempt some types of income soon arises. Indeed, the clamor of interest groups virtually ensures that some types of exemptions will be written into tax laws. Exemptions can easily be justified as providing relief for specific groups that might be excessively burdened by the obligation of a tax, or they might be conceived as a method of equalizing society's haves with its have-nots.

During the early years of the income tax, economists and tax experts argued over the definition of income. Determining precisely how the government would view income when writing tax laws was far from a simple question. Millions of dollars were in the balance. According to some authorities, any workable definition of income for tax purposes must differentiate income from capital. Others argued that the primary task in identifying income was to conceive a definition based on consumption. Still others hoped to define income in terms of productivity. While all of these perspectives of what constitutes true income have to some degree influenced tax law in the United States, the general view that most often prevails defines income as the increase of economic, or purchasing, power an individual possesses over a given period of time. Most commonly, this may be reduced to how much money an individual gains over a given period of time.

In the 1913 Tax Law, legislators settled on a broad definition of income.

> "Gains, profits, and income derived from salaries, wages, or compensation for personal service of whatever kind and in whatever form paid, or from

professions, vocations, businesses, trade, commerce, or sales, or dealings in property, whether real or personal, growing out of the ownership or use of or interest in real or personal property, also from interest, rent, dividends, securities, or the transaction of any lawful business...or gains or profits and income derived from any source whatever..."

The writers of the law clearly did not want to omit any form of income. A key phrase here is "...gains or profits and income derived from any source whatever..." Such a broad, and rather open-ended description of taxable income virtually ensures that all gains, no matter their origination, are taxable. Even if a specific type of gain is not noted, the phrase "from any source whatever..." seems to ensure its inclusion. And this, of course, is merely the starting point.

It soon became obvious that such a broad definition needed to be focused and applied in a manner that the tax code became at least reasonably fair to the majority of citizens. Even during the income tax's formative stages most people recognized that many economic activities clearly constitute income. The factory worker's paycheck for his labor unquestionably is income; the shopkeeper's profits after expenses is income; and the doctor's fee for his services is income. Similarly, the farmer's selling of his crop, the carpenter's payment for building a barn, and the police officer's pay for protecting the public are all forms of income. Other types of economic activity are not so clear-cut, however. Suppose a farmer pays a doctor for curing his ailing child by giving the doctor a portion of his corn crop? Does the corn constitute income? What if the doctor offers free medical service for a year to a carpenter if the carpenter builds him a new porch for the doctor's home? The carpenter gains the equivalent of perhaps hundreds of dollars in fees that would go for medical care, while the doctor gains a new porch, which is certainly a thing of value that can be equated to money.

Stocks and bonds created problems of their own. Consider this example regarding stocks. When the market goes up without fluctuation, it is clear that the owner of the stocks has gained. For example, if he owns 500 shares of stock valued at a dollar per share, and the shares increase in value over a twelve-month period to two dollars per share, he has gained $500 in value. However, what happens if the stock, valued at a dollar per share, decreases to 50 cents per share? He has lost money; but is he entitled to a reduction of his taxes? To complicate matters, what if during the first six months of the year his stock decreases in value, but then regains those losses to end the year at the same value it began. Does this increase now count as a gain? For the early creators of the income tax, such questions proved to be major issues, for no one had experience with formulating income tax policy.

Real estate posed additional problems for early tax theorists. Suppose a man's house increases in value 5% in a given year. The house has certainly gained in value, but does he have income? He has not received any. If he sells the house several years later, how is his gain to be calculated if through the years the rates of income tax have varied? Would he be required to pay the current rate? Or would he be required to figure up his yearly gains and pay tax based on the rates of each year specific gains were achieved? In the former case, if current rates are low, he has paid less in taxes than perhaps he should have? In the latter, calculating the tax due would result in at least a serious computational headache and at the worst major mistakes.

Business income also posed problems. Legislators had to write a tax law that was fair to business, or they risked undermining economic activity. What good would it be to tax a business if the tax forced the company into eventual bankruptcy? Again, in the early period of the income tax legislators had few models on which to base their policies. Business expenses were a major issue. It made sense to most legislators that business expenses should be deducted from a business's gross income. Thus, net profit becomes the basis of the income tax. Figuring net profit is not always so easy, though. What expenses should be deductible? Suppose a business profits on 80% of its manufactured goods, but suffers losses on 20% of its products. Should this 20% be deducted from the business's net profits? Moreover, what if a business assumes a loan for expansion and, because of its overall expansion costs, does not realize a profit? Is the business liable for any income taxes? Can the owner of the business take his losses and apply them against income that he has gained from other enterprises?

Other questions that early income tax experts confronted concerned inheritance and gifts. If inherited money and property were taxable, and if gifts were not taxable, an individual nearing the end of his or her life could simply turn over all of his or her assets to heirs in the form of a gift. In like fashion, if gifts were taxable, should there be any limit, any exemptions? Should a grandparent's monetary gift to a toddler be taxed as income? If not, it would be possible for a wealthy grandparent to transfer assets of great value to a grandchild without tax consequence.

Questions like these and others usually cause little confusion for the modern taxpayer. Over the years the tax laws have been refined, revised, and rewritten so often that they address virtually every income related activity. When the income tax was first passed and the tax code was being formulated, few models of comprehensive tax laws existed and legislators had to design the system. Confusion and errors often resulted from legitimate attempts to make the income tax an effective and equitable method of raising government revenue.

The Call for a Progressive Tax

Although they might have argued over the precise definition of income and haggled over exemptions and deductions, backers of the income tax were united in the overall need for the tax and the need that the tax be progressive. Unquestionably, the idea of an income tax and progressive tax have been and remain closely linked.

The principal forms of a national system of taxation prior to the income tax were tariffs and excise taxes. Because they placed a greater burden on the poor, they were considered to be regressive. Whereas all citizens pay the tax when they buy an imported product, a rich man is hurt less by the tax than a poor man is, because the tax consumes much less of the rich man's overall assets than it does that of a poor man. A progressive, or graduated tax, based on one's ability to pay would in theory make taxes more fair on the overall population.

A flat tax was certainly not the answer, at least to the men designing the early income tax. Ten percent of a poor man's income would leave him with far less purchasing power than a rich man who pays 10% of his income in tax. The poor man's tax obligation is therefore a greater burden than that of the rich man. To make the tax burdens more equitable, a greater percentage of income must be required as one's income increases. Accordingly, to be fair an income tax must be progressive.

The argument might be raised that a progressive tax is unfair, because all people benefit from the operation and activities of government, and if wealthier people pay a progressive rate, they are in essence paying more for government services and thus subsidizing the poor. This point can be easily countered, however, by noting that the rich typically own more property than poor people and thus they benefit more from police, fire protection, national defense, and other essential government services.

Underlying these hotly debated issues was yet another justification. Since poor people spend their income on the necessities of life – food, shelter, and clothing – while the rich were widely perceived to spend their vast incomes on luxuries and nonessentials, many considered a progressive tax to be a social equalizer. A progressive income tax could decrease the economic gap between rich and poor, which much of the public and many legislators felt to be a worthy social goal.

The above views were shared by many proponents of the income tax. To the early designers of the income tax, it was clear: a progressive income tax was the only way to ensure fairness.

Those most affected by a progressive tax quickly raised objections. Most of the arguments revolved around the following:

- Any form of progressive taxation will make tax law difficult to administer.

- Progressive taxation will cause strong resentment and encourage taxpayers to find ways to avoid paying the tax. This could result in the government losing tax revenues.

- Progressive taxation will result in demands for exemptions, which will only complicate the tax law and lead to inequities. This is counter to the intention of a progressive tax.

- A progressive tax will likely lead to abuse on the part of the government. Because a progressive tax would fall most heavily on the wealthy, who constitute a minority in the country, the majority, comprised of poorer taxpayers, through their legislators impose their will on the wealthy minority, regardless of fairness and without sanction.

- A progressive tax will erode economic incentives. When a person feels that the more income he achieves the more taxes he will pay, he eventually will lose his incentive to achieve. After all, why continue to work hard and press ahead if the government takes an ever-expanding portion of your earnings? Ultimately, this argument continues, the nation will suffer an erosion of capital, because the rich invest their wealth, creating capital.

Although somewhat simplified here, these are powerful arguments that continue to raise doubt over the fairness of a progressive tax. Nonetheless, at the time of the income tax's inception, the forces supporting a progressive tax were stronger than those in opposition and a progressive income was soon enacted.

The Case for Exemptions

Once it became clear that there was little possibility of repealing a progressive tax, groups affected by the income tax turned to exemptions. The idea of exemptions was not new. Some of the first voices to raise it were advocates of the poor, who argued that those whose incomes placed them at the poverty level should be exempt from income tax. How could government, in good conscience, demand a part of an individual's income when that individual required his or her entire income to maintain a lifestyle at a subsistence level?

The mere idea of an exemption raised numerous questions, few of them being easy to answer. When considering an exemption for the poor, for example, poverty needed to be defined. What methods or standards could be used to measure it? What if a person had little income but owned much valuable property? Should this person be entitled to an exemption on income? Should other taxes be considered when determining an individual's right to an exemption of income tax? The question of exemptions inevitably led back to the definition of income. Should earned and unearned income be treated differently in regard to exemptions? How should capital gains be treated?

Upon close examination of the problem, the idea of exemptions became thornier. Should consideration be given to married couples where a spouse does not work? Should consideration be given to family size? A single man who earns a particular wage may not be living near the poverty level, but a man earning the same wage who is married and has four children might be. Should this man be given exemptions? However, what happens if the first man, who does not have a family, suffers a serious illness that consumes a large part of his income in a given year? Is he now entitled to an exemption? If yes, at what point does he become eligible? Should major medical bills ever be a cause for an exemption or deduction?

Soon after enactment of the income tax, various groups began to see exemptions and deductions as a way to protect income, or at least retain some control over how their money would be spent. Gifts to charities, for example, if deductible, permit a taxpayer to gain the satisfaction of applying money to a worthy cause, while at the same time reducing taxable income. Certainly this is noteworthy. The charity can then use the money to help the needy.

The overall result of the idea exemptions gave rise to numerous groups who all tried to influence tax policy to reflect their own goals. The struggle over exemptions continues today with Congress revising the tax code to satisfy the most powerful lobbies.

Personal and Corporate Income Taxes

In 1913, Congress changed the excise tax that applied to corporations to an income tax. It seemed to be a logical decision, because corporations enjoy a legal status similar to individuals. Not so logical is the fact that after paying taxes on income a corporation may then distribute dividends to stockholders, who must pay income taxes on the amount of the dividends, making this a form of double taxation. The designers of the income tax were not immediately concerned with such dilemmas, however, as they were in general agreement on the need for an income tax. This was their primary goal; related issues could be dealt with later. Unfortunately, some of these issues are still being debated today.

Setting aside the problem of double taxation, a corporate income tax presented numerous problems. This is especially true of large corporations that enjoy a complex operation. Income may be earned in one year, but, because of the type of business, may be placed on the books in the following year. How is such income taxed if income tax rates change? Is the income taxed during the year it was earned, or the year it is accounted for? The question of losses also looms large. Should a loss be deductible only in the year it occurred, or may it be carried over to the next year? What happens in the case of a loss that results after income has been realized from a particular business activity?

The definition of income continued to be perplexing. Throughout the last quarter of the 19th century and well into the 20th, America experienced explosive industrial growth. Businesses were started by the millions in what was evolving as the world's most diverse economy. To write a simple, yet fair, set of rules regarding how businesses would be taxed was almost impossible. Adding to the confusion were business owners and corporate heads who according to industry began to mobilize and lobby Congress for exemptions and favorable deductions for their specific businesses. As Congress granted exemptions or deductions to one type of business, others demanded the same favors, or treatment equal in kind. The result only complicated the formulation of tax laws.

The federal income tax arose of the desire of progressive legislators to find a way to pay for an expanded role of government that would bring about social reforms and change the federal tax system from one based on tariffs and excise taxes that they felt unfairly burdened the poor. Although originally conceived to be a rather small part of the overall system of federal taxation, the income tax quickly became the dominant tax, growing in reach until today it affects the vast majority of individuals and corporations earning income.

The Evolving Federal Income Tax

Even though the First World War had ended in 1917, income tax rates remained high. The federal government needed money to pay off the debt that had accumulated during the war. Standing at $25 billion in 1919 (up from a mere $1 million in 1916), the debt was a major issue among many of the country's legislators, economists, and particularly taxpayers. For those paying the tax, which was still limited to the affluent, resentment over the rates increased.

This battle between those who would have income tax rates reduced and those who prefer to keep rates high to pay the nation's debt, as well as to fund an increase in the services of government, has been one of the most long-running issues in the income tax controversy. From the 1920s on, tax rates have generally been raised during wars – World War II, the Korean War, and the Vietnam War – and during periods of major economic downturns such as the Great Depression when taxes were increased to provide for more government spending and create jobs. Conversely, rates have generally been lowered during times of calm and prosperity. During the 1920s income tax rates were decreased four times. Other major decreases in income tax rates occurred in 1948, 1962, and 1964. During the 1970s, income tax rates were decreased five times. Throughout the 1980s and 1990s, income tax rates have raised and lowered in response to the demands of various interest groups. From 1981 through 1993, 11 major tax acts were passed by Congress. Virtually every taxpayer in the country was affected.

The Great Rate Debate

By the early 1920s many of those individuals who were required to pay income taxes had grown deeply resentful of a tax system they felt was unfair and confiscatory. They had no galvanizing leader, however, no one capable of focusing the debate and making the reduction of income tax rates a national issue. That changed in 1921 with the appointment of Andrew W. Mellon as Secretary of the Treasury.

Mellon was an industrialist who had amassed a fortune, and he and many of his friends and associates were among those who were paying some of the highest income taxes in the country. He would have liked to eliminate the income tax but realized that was politically impossible; the government had grown too dependent on the tax. Instead, he settled on a goal of reducing income tax rates.

Mellon's plan called for the highest rates to range from 15% to 25%. The taxpayers with the lowest incomes would pay the lowest rates, while those with the highest incomes would pay the highest rates, but no one would pay more than 25%. Mellon believed – as do many people today – that lower rates would spur investment because people would be able to keep more of their income. That income would be invested, providing capital for industrial expansion, which would in turn create jobs, which in turn would lead to a robust economy. Mellon also counseled that when rates are excessive, people find ways to circumvent the laws and avoid paying taxes. When this happens, the government loses revenue. Moreover, according to Mellon, high income taxes undermine business initiative, because entrepreneurs are unwilling to start new ventures when potential rewards are excessively taxed. Why take a business risk if 90% of every dollar you will potentially earn must be paid in tax? Many individuals who call for lower tax rates today still cite Andrew Mellon's arguments in one form or another.

Although Mellon would have liked to reduce the highest income tax rates much lower – his ideal would have been a flat rate of 10% - he was only able to get maximum rates reduced to 56% from 73% in 1921. Nonetheless, this was a significant amount for many individuals. Mellon kept trying and through his efforts the maximum rates were reduced again in 1924 to 46%. In his speeches, Mellon called upon cutting tax rates even more as a means of supporting investment which would create more jobs.

With the Revenue Act of 1926, the maximum individual rate on all income above $100,000 was cut from 46% to 25%. For taxpayers on the lowest end of the scale, the rate was cut from 2% on the first $4,000 of taxable income to 1.5%. Moreover, the maximum estate tax was reduced to 20% from 40%, and gift taxes were abolished.

While many people had expected that the reduced rates would lead to a strong, growing economy, much of the money that would have gone for taxes went instead into the stock market, helping to fuel the wild speculation that led to the Great Depression. Some people blamed the Depression on the tax cuts, however, the Depression resulted from several factors, perhaps most importantly a lack of safeguards and regulation of the securities industry. Certainly the tax cuts alone did not cause the Great Depression.

In an attempt to reverse the decline in economic output and create jobs, income tax rates were raised once again. In

1932 the maximum rates rose to 63% and in 1936 to 79%. As the country slowly climbed out of depression, many economists and tax experts embraced the idea that higher rates were the foundation of the recovery. Of course, the fact remains that the country did not fully emerge from the Great Depression until World War II and its demands for war materials.

Creation of the Modern Income Tax

World War II, unquestionably, was a period of upheaval and chaos – a period when much of Europe and the Pacific was destroyed. While historians often detail the war in terms of the human and social costs, few note that the war directly led to the creation of the current system of income tax in the United States. To pay for the costs brought about by the war effort, virtually every American wage earner was required to pay his or her fair share.

Major tax legislation was passed in the years 1940, 1941, 1942, and 1943. Each one increased the tax burden. Following are the highlights of these tax acts:

- The lowest tax bracket was reduced to $2,000 from $4,000.

- The lowest rates increased from 4% to 19%.

- The maximum rate increased first to 81%, and then to 88%.

- The income level of the top rate was reduced from $5 million to $200,000.

- The personal exemption for married couples was reduced to $1,200 from $2,500.

- In 1943, withholding was passed into law. This was   perhaps one of the most significant changes in the tax law, because the government now collected taxes before the end of the tax year, making it almost impossible for salaried individuals to under-report their income.

The results of the tax legislation were profound and far-reaching. Government revenues from the income tax increased to an astonishing 1,800%, with actual collections increasing from about $1 billion in 1939 to close to $20 billion in 1944. The numbers of individual taxpayers increased ten times, from 4 million in 1939 to 40 million in 1943.

After the war the government's need for revenue continued. Not only did the United States send massive amounts of aid to help other countries rebuild, but the demands of the Cold War and the Korean conflict led to high and sustained spending on defense. There was also the growing consensus, particularly among liberals, that the federal government had a responsibility to foster social welfare and promote equality. The myriad programs initiated with such aims required funds, which in turn led to the growth of bureaucracies, which led to the need for more money. In a spiral that continues today bureaucracies beget more programs which lead to expansion of the bureaucracy, which then leads to more programs. Once begun, the spiral of bureaucracies and programs is difficult to control or stop.

Calls for tax reduction again surfaced, but with a populace tired of war and growing post-war prosperity, most people were more interested in continuing with their lives than worrying about their taxes. It was not until the early 1960s and the Kennedy Administration that the idea of tax reform and a reduction of rates began to regain popularity. Although the debate originally centered around the old argument of rates, once the reforms were passed, a rather new philosophy emerged that focused on the manipulation of the tax system to favor specific groups. While there had always been partisans of various causes in Washington, who were always eager to discuss with legislators the needs of the groups they represented, the sixties witnessed a dramatic increase in the numbers of paid lobbyists. These individuals came to realize that one of the best ways they could help their employers was to convince legislators to revise tax laws so that their employers would benefit. No longer were rates the sole issue, but which types of income would be subject to taxation also gained favor. This, of course, resulted in a proliferation of loopholes in the tax code that affected millions of taxpayers.

In 1964, the major components of the Kennedy tax reform plan were fully initiated. Most importantly, the top rate was reduced to 70% from 91%, but this was only the start of what would be several revisions to the tax laws in the upcoming years.

Taxes in the 1980s and 1990s

Since the early 1980s, taxes have become one of the most hotly debated issues in American politics. From 1981 through 1993 Congress passed 11 major tax acts and the topic of taxes will undoubtedly continue well into the next century.

The year 1981 witnessed one of the largest tax reductions in history for both individuals and businesses. The most important features of the legislation lowered the top income bracket for individuals from 70% to 50% and the maximum tax rate on capital gains from 28% to 20%. In addition, individual retirement accounts were permitted and estate taxes were cut. So substantial were the tax cuts and their effect on revenue collections that many of the reductions of the Tax Act of 1981 were reversed or severely curtailed by the tax acts of 1982 and 1984.

By 1986, a desire to reduce taxes again, as well as simplify the tax code, was gaining in popularity. The Tax Reform Act of 1986 proved to be far-reaching in its effects. More than four million people were no longer required to pay income tax, many tax shelters were eliminated, the tax rates for corporations were increased, and some business deductions were restricted. Following are the chief provisions of the 1986 Tax Reform Act:

- The number of tax brackets was reduced to two from 15. The new brackets had rates of 15% and 28%, with a 5% surcharge. The highest rate, therefore, was 33%, significantly reduced from the previous top rate of 50%.

- Personal exemptions and the standard deduction were increased.

- Long-term capital gains were now taxed as other income and at the same rates.

- The deduction for interest on home mortgages was limited to two homes per taxpayer.

- Sales taxes and interest on consumer debt such as credit cards and car loans were no longer deductible.

- Various other deductions were restricted, including those for medical expenses, individual retirement accounts, and interest of money borrowed for investment.

Despite the significant revisions of the federal income tax code that resulted from the 1986 Tax Reform Act, by 1990 calls for further changes were being heard throughout the country. In an attempt to rectify what some considered to be the inequities of the previous reforms, the 1990 Tax Act was aimed at the rich and restricted and in many cases eliminated personal benefits and deductions regularly taken by affluent taxpayers. The 1990 Act also placed luxury taxes on expensive cars, jewelry, furs, boats, and planes.

A major goal of the tax reformers of the 1990s was to adjust the tax code so that the so-called rich shouldered more of the tax burden. In the 1993 Tax Act, a bracket of 36% was added, along with a 10% surtax for the highest income levels. Some business expenses were further limited, and the amount of pension contributions affluent taxpayers could make was also limited. Although some of the luxury taxes of the 1990 Tax Act were repealed, the one on expensive cars remained.

As the United States heads into the new century, taxes are one of the issues most discussed by politicians, legislators, and the public. Calls for tax reform continue and arguments over taxes accompany every budget bill before Congress.

The Modern Driving Forces of the Federal Income Tax

The tax business has grown increasingly sophisticated over the years. When the federal income tax was first implemented, most people viewed it as a means of government revenue. A few recognized that it could become a powerful tool of social engineers, but no one at the time envisioned how vast and comprehensive the federal tax code would one day be.

Various factors influence the shape and scope of the modern income tax. These factors can be broken down into the three major categories:

- Expenses of government, including general operating costs, defense, foreign aid, debt service, and miscellaneous programs (often added by politicians to the budget.)

- Economic considerations, including manipulation of the money supply in an attempt to control inflation and efforts of stimulating or cooling business activity.

- Social considerations, including Social Security, healthcare, education, welfare, unemployment, crime, and numerous other programs deemed to directly benefit society.

These various factors are constantly being balanced against each other in the tax debate. Economists, legislators, and social leaders regularly express their opinions about taxes, even if their opinions lack merit. Consequently, tax policy often emerges from a cauldron of conflicting ideas and compromises and seldom delivers genuine reform or lives up to its promise.

This is easily proven by reviewing the overall tax burden on Americans over the past 30 years. While the government's collection of tax dollars has unquestionably risen over the past few decades, the actual tax burden on American taxpayers has remained relatively constant. In 1968, for example, federal taxes accounted for 18.1% of the country's GDP, while in 1993, federal taxes accounted for 18.6% of the GDP. Although the overall amount of taxes collected as a percent of the tax-paying public has been relatively consistent, the sources of tax revenue have varied. When legislators decrease the rate of one type of tax, they invariably raise the rate of another. Thus, you might pay a lower rate on your income tax, but you will then likely pay more for Social Security or Medicare taxes, which is precisely what happened in the 1980s.

During the 1990s federal income tax has accounted for roughly 60% of federal revenue. Of that, personal income taxes account for about 50% and corporate income taxes about 10%. Social Security taxes have accounted for an additional 35%, translating to a total of about 95% of the federal government's total revenues.

Clearly, the income tax has dramatically changed the way the federal government obtains funds to operate since the days before the income tax when revenues depended on tariffs and excise taxes. It is also clear that until the creation of another revenue generator – perhaps a value added tax – the federal income tax is here to stay.

Do the Rich Really Pay Their Fair Share?

One of the continuing controversies that has surrounded the income tax since its inception has been the question of whether the affluent contribute to their "fair" share of the tax burden. Although the word "fair" has never been defined in a way that everyone accepts, a review of tax records indicates that except for a few periods, the wealthiest Americans have shouldered the greatest percentage of the nation's taxes. There are exceptions, of course, in which some rich taxpayers manage to legally escape taxes, but on the whole those of means tend to account for the greatest portion of federal revenues.

Tax revenues of the 1990s make this quite clear. Consider these average figures:

- The top 1% of U.S. taxpayers accounted for 25% of the federal income taxes paid.

- The top 5% accounted for slightly over 40% of the federal income taxes paid.

- The top 10% accounted for close to 55% of the federal income taxes paid.

- The top 25% accounted for about 75% of the federal income taxes paid.

- The top 50% of the taxpayers accounted for over 90% of the federal income taxes paid.

Unquestionably, the reality of progressive taxation significantly affects the well off. Feeling the burden of the income tax, many affluent taxpayers seek shelters and deductions which can protect their assets and limit their exposure to taxes. Indeed, thousands of affluent Americans pay less taxes than average in their income brackets by taking advantage of a variety of legal strategies, including tax-exempt income, substantial deductions for home mortgage interest, and losses due to casualties and medical expenses. Many have also taken advantage of foreign tax havens, jurisdictions found throughout the world that offer investors various tax incentives. In some tax havens, astute financial strategies and the appropriate investments enable individuals to live tax-free.

Few people would argue that an income tax, or other form of national taxation, is essential for a country to become a strong, vital member of the modern world society. However, when that income tax becomes burdensome, is administered unfairly, or supports wasteful, unnecessary government programs, taxpayers are right to question its validity and seek ways to legitimately reduce their tax obligations.

Tax Havens of the West

A tax haven is a country, enclave, or jurisdiction that encourages investment through a variety of tax incentives. These incentives might be in the form of exemptions of specific taxes, low rates, or tax holidays. Through the strategic use of tax havens, it is possible to significantly reduce your tax exposure and in some cases eliminate tax consequences entirely. While there are places that promote themselves as tax havens and which in fact are dubious investment schemes that benefit only the backers of the scheme, legitimate tax havens are found throughout the world. Investing in them is fully legal as are the tax savings derived from them.

This chapter focuses on some of the best tax havens in the West, which for the purposes of this book includes North America, South America, Europe, and the islands that lie between these land masses. Not only do many of the following tax havens offer numerous methods through which tax reduction can be achieved, many of them offer a superior lifestyle and vast business opportunities as well.

Antigua and Barbuda

Antigua, Barbuda, and Redonda (a rocky uninhabited islet) are an island country in the West Indies, east-southeast of Puerto Rico. Together, the islands have an area of about 150 square miles (440 square kilometers). The islands are mostly flat and low-lying, though Boggy Peak on Antigua is slightly over 1,300 feet in elevation (about 400 meters). The islands lie in the tropical zone.

About 66,000 people live on the islands, with most having descended from Africans, British, and Portuguese. English is the official language, and British influence is found just about everywhere. Although not as well known or glitzy as some of the islands of the Caribbean, Antigua and Barbuda offer a quality lifestyle.

Investment and Taxes

Tourism is the mainstay of the islands' economy, however, transportation, communications, and various types of trade are also important. The infrastructure of the islands is solid. Of most interest to those seeking methods through which to reduce their tax burden is that the islands do not tax personal income.

Contact:

Antigua and Barbuda Dept. of Tourism and Trade
25 S.E. 2nd Ave.
Suite 300
Miami, FL 33131
Tel: 305-381-6762
Fax: 305-381-7908

Antigua and Barbuda Dept. of Tourism and Trade
610 Fifth Ave.
Suite 311
New York, NY 10020
Tel: 212-541-4117
Fax: 212-757-1607

Antigua and Barbuda Dept. of Tourism and Trade
60 Claire Ave., E.
Suite 304
Toronto, Ontario
Canada M4T 1N5
Tel: 416-961-3085
Fax: 416-961-7218

Antigua and Barbuda Dept. of Tourism
Long and Thames Streets
P.O. 363
St. John's
Antigua, W.I.
Tel: 268-462-0480
Fax: 268-462-2483

Antigua and Barbuda
Chief of Mission
3216 New Mexico Ave., NW
Washington, D.C. 20016
Tel: 202-362-5211, 5166, 5122
Fax: 202-362-5225

Anguilla

Anguilla is a small, low-lying island positioned at the northern end of the Leeward Islands in the Caribbean Sea. A British dependency, the island enjoys internal self-government. Anguilla has a total area of about 35 square miles (90 square kilometers) and a tropical, semiarid climate.

The island possesses several miles of spectacular beaches and in recent years has emerged as an important, if not well known, tourist destination. Many who have visited it describe the island as a place offering a relaxing, unhurried pace of life. Anguilla has only about 10,000 residents, most of whom are of African descent. English is the official language, and British influence is apparent. The island's infrastructure is maintained by the British and is of high quality.

Economy and Taxes

Tourism provides the bulk of Anguilla's economy. It also provides much of the island government's revenues. Taxes placed on hotels, imports, the sale of land to foreigners, a lottery, and British aid provide enough to pay for the government's expenses. Consequently, Anguilla offers a variety of significant tax advantages, including:

- There is no income tax.

- There are no corporate taxes.

- There are no sales taxes.

- There are no taxes on capital gains.

- There is no value added tax.

- There are no taxes on interest.

Contact:

The Anguilla Tourist Board
World Trade Centre
Suite 250
San Francisco, CA 94111
Tel: 415-398-3231
Fax: 415-398-3669

The Anguilla Tourist Board
P.O. Box 1388
The Valley
Anguilla
Tel: 809-497-2759 or 800-553-4939
Fax: 809-497-2710

Barbados

Barbados is located in the Windward Islands of the Lesser Antilles. It is the most easterly of the islands in the Caribbean and has an area of about 165 square miles (430 square kilometers). The island lies within the tropical zone, but its temperatures are moderated by the Northeast Trade Winds. The island's picturesque scenery, abundant sunshine, and friendly people make it a prime tourist site.

The resident population of Barbados is about 260,000, of which about 90% are descended from Africans. Whites and individuals of mixed ethnicity comprise the rest. Large numbers of tourists may be found on the island throughout the year. The people of Barbados enjoy a high standard of living, have a literacy rate of 98%, and one of the best per capita income levels of the Caribbean. English is the official language of the island. The island's infrastructure is modern and of high quality.

Boredom is seldom an issue in Barbados. The island's beaches are known for their beauty, and watersports are enjoyed year-round. The island possesses fine hotels, restaurants, and theater groups.

Economy and Taxes

An independent island, Barbados remains a member of the British Commonwealth, enjoying the status and advantages close association with England bestows. Unlike many islands of the Caribbean, Barbados is quite stable. The island's stability and democratic traditions – inherited from Great Britain – have enabled it to focus on development of its economy. In recent years, Barbados has emerged as a major telecommunications and financial center in the Caribbean.

In an ongoing effort of attracting investment, the government of the island has passed legislation that offers important tax incentives. Although many of the incentives are designed for companies that wish to expand their operations to the island, individuals can also benefit from Barbados's tax laws.

An individual's tax status in Barbados is directly dependent upon his or her compliance with the concepts of "resident" and "domiciled." Anyone who is resident and domiciled in Barbados is obligated to pay income tax on his or her income earned throughout the world. This can result in a hefty tax bill. To qualify as an island resident, a person must be present in Barbados for more than 182 days in a tax year. If you are present in Barbados for more than 182 days, but you are not domiciled in Barbados, you are obligated to pay tax on income derived from Barbados, and also on any income earned elsewhere that is remitted to the island. This, too, can be a sizable tax bill. Nonresidents – those who are present on the island for 182 days or less in a tax year – are obligated to pay tax only on income derived from Barbados. With the generous tax incentives provided by the island government, tax on such income is likely to be greatly reduced from what it would be in other jurisdictions.

Because of the government's desire to encourage investment, tax incentives are aimed at those individuals interested in establishing a presence in the business sector. Following is a summary of the incentives included in the island's tax laws.

Significant business incentives (noted in the International Business Companies Act 1991-24) are detailed in the island's tax legislation, including:

- A tax rate of 2.5% on profits.

- Exemptions from all local taxes on dividends, interest, fees, royalties, management fees, and other incomes paid to non-residents.

- Exemptions from taxes and duties on machinery, raw   materials, computer equipment, and other items and materials imported into Barbados for business purposes.

- Exemptions from local taxes on transfers of assets or securities, except in cases of transfer of real property located in Barbados or for equipment used on the island.

- Exemptions from exchange controls.

- A guarantee of the above benefits for a period of 15 years.

Special incentives are offered to companies that provide information services, including:

- A tax rate of 2.5% on profits for those companies specializing in data entry and whose business concentrates on international markets.

- Exemptions from import tariffs on equipment related for production.

Incentives are offered to companies in the manufacturing and export sectors, including:

- An tax exemption on corporate profits for a period of up to 10 years. (Note that upon expiration of the exemption, export industries may be entitled to a tax rate of 2.5%.)

- An exemption from import duties on equipment and raw materials.

International service companies engaged in offshore operations in Barbados are offered a variety of incentives, including:

- A tax rate of 1% to 2.5% on the profits of investment companies.

- A tax rate of 2.5% for international business companies.

- A tax rate of 2.5% on the profits of companies whose operations focus on technology service.

- A full tax exemption for companies defined as "captive insurance companies," as well as a full tax exemption for U.S. foreign sales corporations.

In addition to these various tax incentives, Barbados offers numerous other incentives. Specific businesses may benefit from the following:

- Cash grants for training of staff and workforce.

- Full and unrestricted repatriation of capital, profits, and dividends.

- Simplified customs procedures.

- Subsidies for space in one of the island's industrial parks.

- The possibility of accelerated allowance for depreciation.

- Free assistance with the procedures for investment in the island, decreasing bureaucratic red tape.

Contact:

Barbados Investment and Development Corporation
800 Second Ave.
New York, NY 10017
Tel: 212-867-6420
Fax: 212-682-5496

Barbados Investment and Development Corporation
5160 Yonge St.
Suite 1800
North York, Ontario MN2 6L9
Tel: 416-512-0700
Fax: 416-512-6580

Barbados Investment and Development Corporation
Princess Alice Highway
Bridgetown, Barbados
West Indies
Tel: 809-427-5350
Fax: 809-426-7802

The Bahamas

The Bahamas are an extensive island group beginning some 50 miles (80 kilometers) from Florida's east coast. Of the several thousand small islets and cays, only thirty are inhabited, with Nassau being one of the best known. The island group, which stretches from Florida to about 60 miles (96 kilometers) from Cuba, covers over 100,000 square miles (260,000 square kilometers) of ocean, yet the total area of The Bahamas is only 5,400 squares miles (13,900 square kilometers). The islands enjoy a delightful climate throughout the year, with great amounts of sunshine and average high temperatures of near 80° F (27° C).

Slightly more than 270,000 people live on the islands, however, the population is always higher because of tourists. The Bahamas are truly one of the world's prime locations, offering a wonderful lifestyle in a tropical setting. Although The Bahamas enjoy internal self-government, they remain a part of the British Commonwealth and ties to England are strong. English is the principal language and British influence is found throughout the islands. The lifestyle one can achieve in The Bahamas is one of the finest in the Caribbean.

Economy and Taxes

Tourism, banking and financial services, pharmaceuticals, and the production of rum are important components of the economy of the Bahamas, with tourism alone accounting for close to half of the islands' GDP. It is noteworthy that the chief source of government revenue comes from import duties, licensing fees for business, stamp duties, and departure tax. It is also noteworthy that the government of The Bahamas has not entered into any tax treaties with other countries.

In an attempt to encourage investment, The Bahamas also offer numerous tax benefits, including:

- There is no personal income tax.

- There is no corporate income tax.

- There is no tax on dividends.

- There is no tax on capital gains.

- There is no tax on interest.

- There is no tax on interest.

- There is no tax on royalties.

- There is no sales tax.

- There is no payroll tax.

- There is no tax on gifts.

- There is no death duty for real or personal estates, nor succession, estate, or inheritance taxes.

Contact:

The Bahamas Tourism Office
150 E. 52nd St.
28 Floor North
New York, NY 10022
Tel: 212-758-2777
Fax: 212-753-6531

The Bahamas Tourism Office
P.O. Box N 3701
Nassau
The Bahamas
Tel: 242-322-7500
Fax: 242-328-0945

Bermuda

Bermuda, a group of a some 150 islands, is located in the North Atlantic Ocean, east of North Carolina. Only about 20 of the islands are inhabited, and of these, Great Bermuda is the most populated and well known. When most people speak of Bermuda, they are actually talking about Great Bermuda. The Bermudan Islands have an overall area of about 20 square miles and lie mostly near or slightly above sea level. All of the islands enjoy a subtropical climate that is mild and relatively humid. The climate, known for its delightful sunshine, makes Bermuda a popular vacation site.

The islands have about 62,000 year-round residents, however there are always thousands of tourists present. A dependent territory of the United Kingdom, English is the predominate language and British influence is found throughout the islands. Health care, education, and infrastructure are all of high quality.

Bermuda is one of the most affluent and prosperous jurisdictions in the world. Its GDP per capita of $28,000 is among the world's highest, and the lifestyle it offers its residents and visitors is exceptional.

Economy and Taxes

While most people think of Bermuda as primarily a vacation destination, the islands' economic foundation is far broader than just the tourist industry. Bermuda is also recognized for its financial services, ship repair, and pharmaceuticals. The island government also provides numerous and generous tax advantages, including the following:

- There is no income tax.

- There are no personal taxes.

- There are no taxes on corporate profits.

- There are no taxes on personal or corporate dividends.

- There are no capital gains tax.

- There are no withholding taxes.

- There are no gift taxes.

- There are no inheritance taxes.

Companies may also benefit from tax incentives. International companies registered in Bermuda may apply for an exemption from taxes on profits or income until the year 2016 in the event that such taxes are ever implemented in Bermuda. Such companies may be fully owned by individuals who are not Bermudan.

The only drawback for some individuals to benefiting from Bermuda's tax incentives is the cost of settling in the islands and the difficulty of obtaining a residency permit. In most cases, a resident is required to buy property in the islands that is valued at least one million dollars. Given that Bermuda is as close to a true tropical paradise as one can get, and considering its history of stability, minimal government bureaucracy, and lack of exchange controls, the cost of residency might not be so high after all.

Contact:

The Bermuda Department of Tourism
205 E. 42nd St.
16th Floor
New York, NY 10017
Tel: 212-818-9800 or 800-223-6106

Bermuda Department of Tourism
245 Peachtree Center, Ave., NE
Suite 803
Atlanta, GA 30303
Tel: 404-524-1541
Fax: 404-586-9933

Bermuda Department of Tourism
1200 Bay St.
Suite 1004
Toronto, M5R 2A5
Canada
Tel: 416-923-9600 or 800-387-1304 (inside Canada)
Fax: 416-923-4840

The Bermuda Tourism Office
Global House
43 Church St.
Hamilton, HM 11
Bermuda
Tel: 441-292-0023
Fax: 441-292-7537

Cayman Islands

The Cayman Islands, comprised of Grand Cayman, Little
Cayman, and Cayman Brac, are located in the Caribbean Sea
about halfway between Cuba and Honduras. The low-lying

islands are small with a total area of about 100 square miles (260 kilometers). They possess a tropical marine climate with somewhat rainy summers and dryer winters.

About 35,000 people reside on the Cayman Islands, although tourists and vacationers visit throughout the year. Indeed with their marvelous beaches and high standard of living, the islands are a popular destination. As a dependency of Great Britain, the Cayman Islands maintain close ties with the British, who have maintained a modern infrastructure over the years. English, of course, is the main language and British influence and customs are found throughout the islands.

Economy and Taxes

The Cayman Islands offer their people one of the highest standards of living in the world. With close to one million visitors each year, tourism is a major part of the islands' economy, however, the islands are also known as one of the world's leading offshore financial centers. Numerous major banks and financial services companies are represented in the Cayman Islands. To encourage investment, the island government offers important tax incentives, including:

• There is no income tax.

- There is no other direct taxation of any kind

Contact:

Cayman Islands Department of Tourism
420 Lexington Ave.
Suite 2733
New York, NY 10170
Tel: 212-682-5582
Fax: 212-986-5123

Cayman Islands Department of Tourism
6100 Blue Lagoon Dr.
Suite 150
Miami, FL 33126-2085
Tel: 305-266-2300
Fax: 305-267-2932

Cayman Islands Department of Tourism
3440 Wilshire Blvd.
Suite 1202
Los Angeles, CA 90010
Tel: 213-738-1968
Fax: 213-738-1829

Cayman Islands Department of Tourism
9525 W. Bryn Mawr
Suite 160
Rosemont, IL 60018
Tel: 847-678-6446
Fax: 847-678-6675

Department of Tourism
P.O. Box 67
George Town
Grand Cayman, BWI
Tel: 345-949-0623
Fax: 345-949-4053

Ecuador

Although not always associated with the premier tax havens around the world, Ecuador offers several tax incentives that for some individuals can result in major benefits. The smallest of the Andean countries, Ecuador is located in northwestern South America. The country, with an area of about 110,000 square miles (285,000 square kilometers), possesses varying terrain from coastal lowlands to great mountains and dense jungles. Cotopaxi, the nation's highest point at 19,347 feet (5,897 meters), is the world's tallest active volcano. Although Ecuador lies over the equator, its different elevations ensure that its climate varies. Jungle lowlands are steamy and hot while temperatures in the higher mountains are cooler. Ecuador is a land of wondrous natural beauty.

Ecuador's population of 11.5 million is comprised of Mestizos, Native Americans, Spanish, and blacks. The country's official language is Spanish, but several Indian dialects are also spoken, mostly in remote areas. While a superior quality of life can be had in the major cities, the standard of living falls as one moves into the countryside. The country's infrastructure, similarly, is most modern in the cities.

Economy and Taxes

Ecuador possesses significant reserves of oil, which has increased its role in the country's economy. Ecuador also has abundant mineral resources, but much of its mineral wealth is located in remote regions and is difficult to mine. Agriculture is another important sector of the economy with bananas, coffee, rice, and sugar being major export products.

Ecuador is recognized for its low cost of living compared to North America and Western Europe. Homes, food, and services in Ecuador are extremely reasonable by Western standards.

In an effort to encourage foreign investment the Ecuadorian government treats foreign and domestic investors equally, and also offers several tax incentives, including:

- There is no tax on income originating from foreign sources. This includes (but is not restricted to) income from interest, dividends, and pensions.

- There are no provincial taxes, county taxes, or municipal taxes in Ecuador.

- There are no taxes on inheritance, gifts, or donations, except in regard to assets located in Ecuador.

- Capital gains are taxed at a rate of 8%.

- For income derived from Ecuadorian sources, income tax rates are quite modest compared to the rates of other countries.

It should also be noted that all investors are permitted to participate in the Andean Common Market without any restrictions. In addition, both foreign and local investors have easy access to foreign exchange for the remission of profits and repatriation of their investments.

Contact:

Consulate of Ecuador
800 Second Ave.
Suite 601

New York, NY 10017
Tel: 212-808-0170 or 212-808-0171
Fax: 212-808-0188

Consulate of Ecuador
B.I.V. Tower
1101 Brickelle Ave.
Suite M-102
Miami, FL 33131
Tel: 305-539-8214/15
Fax: 305-539-8313

Consulate of Ecuador
500 North Michigan Ave.
Suite 1510
Chicago, IL 60611
Tel: 312-329-0266
Fax: 312-329-0359

Consulate of Ecuador
Wilshire Blvd.
Suite 540
Los Angeles, CA 90211
Tel: 323-658-6020
Fax: 323-658-1934

Consulate of Ecuador
151 Bloor St., West
Suite 470
Toronto, Ontario
Canada M5S 1S4
Tel: 416-968-2077
Fax: 416-968-3348

Guatemala

Guatemala lies just south of Mexico and stretches across Central America, giving it access to both the Pacific and Atlantic Ocean. Much of the country's area of 42,000 square miles (108,800 square kilometers) is comprised of highlands and mountains. Although the country lies well within the tropics, it possesses numerous climates based on elevation. Lowland areas are humid and hot; highlands and mountainous regions are dryer and cooler.

Of the country's 11 million people, most are either Mestizos or descended from Native Americans. Spanish is the official language, with about 60% of the population speaking it, while the remainder of the people speak any of several Indian dialects. An enjoyable standard of living is attainable in Guatemala City, the capital, however, much of the country is poor and underdeveloped.

Economy and Taxes

Throughout its history, Guatemala's economy has been rather weak, but many consider the country to possess the potential for growth. Tourism is growing, with visitors seeking the nation's beaches and overall ecological beauty. A pro-business environment has grown in recent years and a free-market climate is prevalent. Most importantly, there are no limitations on foreign investment or foreign ownership of businesses or corporations. Moreover, there are no restrictions on repatriation of capital.

To support the growth of businesses, Guatemala has established free trade zones that offer numerous tax benefits. Incentives vary according to the type of company and business sector, including:

- For companies located within a free trade zone and which are engaged in commercial activities –

  - An exemption from taxes, duties, or import charges on commodities and components stored in the zone for use in commerce and trade.

  - A five-year exemption of tax on income gained from commercial activities that take place within the zone.

  - An exemption of value added tax on goods transferred inside and between free trade zones within Guatemala.

• For companies operating in the free trade zone and that engage in service and manufacturing –

> - A 12-year exemption of tax on income gained from the manufacture or providing of services arising from operations within the zone.

> - A tax exemption on the import of equipment, tools, machinery, containers, packaging, and raw materials needed by the company for its operations.

> - An exemption of value added tax on goods transferred between free trade zones in the country.

• For companies involved in the tourist sector –

> - An exemption from all duties and import taxes on all materials and equipment needed for the business that is not produced in Guatemala or another Central American country.

> - An exemption from real estate taxes on new construction and the expansion and improvement of existing structures and facilities.

The manner in which the income tax is calculated according to the Guatemalan tax code may also benefit some investors. Although income tax is based on gross income, there are many notable exclusions, including:

- Interest from bonds or titles of government.

- Dividends.

- Any benefits which have already been taxed in in another form for the same tax period.

As a means of assisting individuals who are considering investing in Guatemala, the Guatemalan Development Foundations, FUNDESA, has created the Guatemala Business Center (GBC). The GBC is designed to make investment in the country practical and efficient. The staff of the GBC offers up-to-date information on the business environment of the country, recommends contact people, agencies, and professionals who can be of further aid, and can even help with scheduling visits to the country.

Contact:

The Guatemala Business Center
1001 Howard Ave.
Plaza Tower, Suite 2504
New Orleans, LA 70113
Tel: 504-558-3750 or 800-794-GUAT
Fax: 504-558-3755

The Guatemala Business Center
7231 SW 63rd Ave.
Suite 101
South Miami, FL 33143
Tel: 305-666-0066 or 800-741-6133
Fax: 305-666-0570

The Guatemalan Development Foundation
Diagonal 6, 10-65 Zona 10
Centro Gerencial Las Margaritas, Torre I, Oficina 402
Guatemala
Central America
Tel: 502-332-7952 through 56
Fax: 502-332-7958

Honduras

Honduras is another Central American country that, like Guatemala, offers various tax incentives in an effort to encourage investment. Also like Guatemala, Honduras is relatively small with an area of 43,277 square miles (112,090 square kilometers), and has varying topography and climates. Along the coasts the weather remains tropical throughout the year, but becomes a bit cooler and dryer in the mountains which in some places stretch upward to about 9,000 feet (2,800 meters). Volcanoes and impressive valleys are found throughout the country.

Honduras has about 5.6 million people, of which close to 90% are Mestizos with the rest comprised of Indians, blacks, and Europeans. Spanish is the country's official language, but English is common among the educated, particularly in Tegucigalpa, the capital. Several Indian languages are also spoken, though these are generally confined to remote regions. Although Honduras is one of the poorer countries of Central America, a quality lifestyle can be enjoyed in the capital.

Economy and Taxes

Despite the government's efforts at building a pro-business environment and strong economy, Honduras still lags behind many of its neighbors in economic output. However, several factors promise future growth. The overall infrastructure is good, and the telecommunications industry is rapidly modernizing. Puerto Cortes is the only deep water port in Central America and it is also one of the region's most modern. The country's financial system is expanding rapidly and includes several major banks, four international airports serve the capital, and the Honduras produces enough electricity so export to its neighbors.

To encourage investment the government has developed several Free Trade Zones and Export Processing Zones (EPZ). Companies operating within the Inhdelva Free Trade Zone, for example, enjoy the following benefits:

- There is no federal income tax.

- There is no state income tax.

- There are no corporate taxes.

- There are no local taxes.

- There are no sales taxes.

- There are no duties charged on the import of equipment or machinery, parts, raw materials, and supplies that are necessary to a company's operations.

- There is a full exemption from export duties, fees, and controls.

In addition, companies that operate within the zone enjoy currency conversion without restriction and they may withdraw capital or profit without restriction. They also enjoy various programs which enable them to ship certain products duty-free to North America.

Companies that operate in an Export Processing Zone are also eligible for incentives, most notably an exemption from taxes for as long as the company remains in the zone.

Contact:
Consulate General of Honduras
80 Wall St.
Suite 915
New York, NY 10005
Tel: 212-269-3611

Consulate General of Honduras
1707 N. Burling St.
Chicago, IL 60614
Tel: 312-951-6382
Fax: 312-951-6394

Miami Consulate of Honduras
300 Sevilla Ave.
Suite 201
Coral Gables, FL 33134
Tel: 305-447-8927

Consulate General of Honduras
3450 Wilshire Blvd.
Suyite 235
Los Angeles, CA 90010
Tel: 305-383-9244

Economic Dept., Embassy of Honduras
3007 Tilden St., N.W.

P.O. Drawer 4M
Washington, D.C. 20008
Tel: 202-966-7702
Fax: 202-966-9751

General Directorate of Export and Investment
Promotion
4to. Piso. Edificio Salame
Tegucigalpa
Honduras
Central America
Tel: 504-37-1850
Fax: 504-37-8138

Honduran-American Chamber of Commerce
Hotel Honduras Maya Ap. Postal 1838
Tegucigalpa
Honduras
Tel: 504-32-7043
Fax: 504-32-2031

Tegucigalpa Industrial Chamber of Commerce
P.O. Box 3444
Boulevard Centroamerica
Tegucigalpa
Honduras
Tel: 504-32-6803
Fax: 504-31-2049

The Republic of Ireland

The Republic of Ireland should not be confused with Northern Ireland. Although the two share the island of Ireland, the Republic of Ireland is an independent nation while Northern Ireland remains a part of Great Britain. Because of the on-going tensions between Protestants and Catholics, Northern Ireland garners much of the world's news headlines, overshadowing the Republic of Ireland that has quietly emerged as a haven of investment and tax incentives.

The Republic of Ireland covers the greater part of the island of Ireland with an area of about 27,000 square miles (about 70 square kilometers). Northern Ireland has an area of about 5,500 square miles (10,110 square kilometers). The coast varies, being relatively flat in the east and characterized by islets and steep cliffs in the west. The climate of the island is about 25° F (14° C) warmer than one would expect to find at its northern position because of the effects of the Gulf Stream, a mild ocean current that washes over the island's shores. Originating in the tropical waters south of the United States, then flowing along the eastern coast and then across the North Atlantic to Europe, the Gulf Stream warms the atmosphere above it, moderating Ireland's temperatures. The island's average summer temperatures range between 57° and

68° F (about 14° to 20° C) with winter temperatures averaging between 40° and 45° F (about 7° to 14° C).

About 3.7 million people live in the Republic of Ireland, with about one-third living in and around Dublin, the capital and largest city. Most of the population has descended from the Celts, an ancient group of people thought to have originated in Europe and spread throughout the continent and British Isles. An English minority is also present. English and Irish (Gaelic) are the country's official languages. English is most commonly spoken. The standard of living in the Republic of Ireland is comparable to most of the other countries that belong to the European Union, and the country's infrastructure and telecommunications systems are modern and advanced. The Republic of Ireland is a beautiful nation, considered by many to be one of the most pollution-free countries of Europe, if not the world.

Economy and Taxes

The government of the Irish Republic has taken various steps over the last several years to promote the country's economy. Policies to promote the growth of light industry, tourism, and the financial sector have centered around substantial tax incentives, available to both residents and foreigners. The following facts demonstrate the overall strength of the Irish Republic's economy:

- The Republic of Ireland has only about 1% of the European Union's population, but attracts nearly 25% of U.S. investment in manufacturing in Europe.

- Over the last 20 years, 40% of inward investment in the electronics sector of Europe has been targeted for Ireland.

- Of the ten largest software companies in the world, five have development or production facilities in Ireland, which produces close to 60% of all the software sold in Europe.

- Of the world's top 15 pharmaceutical companies, 13 maintain research and development and/or production facilities on the island.

- The Dublin International Financial Services Center has emerged as the favored location within the EU for the financial services industry.

Truly impressive growth has occurred in the country's financial services sector over the past ten to fifteen years. Indeed, the Irish Republic has become a leading financial services center, with Dublin being recognized as a major center for international offshore funds management in Europe. The nation's financial services sector includes various banks, investment and funds companies, credit companies, and credit unions. The many companies of this sector offer investors numerous services, including international banking, funds management, asset finance, and insurance.

A cursory look at the tax code of the Republic of Ireland reveals that the country charges various taxes, including income tax. A closer look, however, makes it clear that major tax incentives are provided.

- Foreign income (except income from the United Kingdom) is not taxable for non-domiciled residents, unless the income is remitted to Ireland.

- Non-residents are not subject to withholding tax on interest payments they receive from a financial services company located at the Customs House Docks Area in Dublin.

- Manufacturing companies may be eligible for a 10% corporate tax rate. (The normal rate is 40%). For qualifying companies, the 10% rate is available until the year 2010.

- International financial services companies located in Dublin may be eligible for a 10% tax rate on profits derived from certified activities. In addition they may be eligible for a 10-year exemption on local property taxes, a 100% write-off for expenditures for new equipment during the first year of operation, a 100% write-off for the costs of new facilities in the first year for owners who occupy their sites, and a 54% write-off for new building costs in the first year for lessors. Companies may also be eligible to enjoy freedom of withholding tax in the payment of interest to recipients.

• Companies granted permission to conduct their operations in the Shannon Airport Customs Free Zone may be eligible for a tax rate of 10% through December of 2005.

Contact:

The Irish Industrial Development Authority
17ᵗʰ Floor
345 Park Ave.
New York, NY 10154
Tel: 212-750-4300
Fax: 212-750-7357

The Irish Industrial Development Authority
The Statler Building
20 Park Plaza
Suite 520
Boston, MA 02116
Tel: 617-484-8225
Fax: 617-338-4745

The Irish Industrial Development Authority
P.O. Box 190129
Atlanta, GA 31119-0129
Tel: 770-351-8474
Fax: 770-351-8568

The Irish Industrial Development Authority
75 E. Wacker Drive
Suite 600
Chicago, IL 60601-3708
Tel: 312-236-0222
Fax: 312-236-3407

The Irish Industrial Development Authority
1620 26th St.
Suite 480 South
Santa Monica, CA 90404
Tel: 310-829-0081
Fax: 310-829-1586

The Irish Industrial Development Authority
Wilton Park House
Wilton Place
Dublin 2
Ireland
Tel: 00-353-0-1-603-4000
Fax: 00-353-0-1-603-4040

The Irish Tourist Board
345 Park Ave.
New York, NY 10154
Tel: 212-418-0800 or 800-223-6470
Fax: 212-371-9052

The Irish Tourist Board
Baggot Street Bridge
Dublin 8
Ireland
Tel: +353-1-602-4000
Fax: +353-1-602-4000

The Irish Embassy in the U.S.
2234 Massachusetts Ave., NW
Washington, D.C. 20008
Tel: 202-462-3939 or 202-462-3940
Fax: 202-232-5993

Madeira

Madeira, often referred to as the "Pearl of the Atlantic," is the largest island of a group of islands located near the Atlantic's prime shipping lanes, about 625 miles from Lisbon and 545 miles from Africa. Overall, the island group has an area of about 286 square miles (740 square kilometers). Although the islands are actually a part of Portugal, forming the district of Funchal, they are an autonomous region. The island government has taken advantage of this status over the years to draft legislation that has promoted the diversification of local industry and encouraged investment through a variety of tax incentives.

Madeira enjoys a mild Mediterranean climate with no extremes of temperature and precipitation. Add scenic beauty to its fine weather and it is easy to understand why tourism has become a prime sector of the island's economy. Indeed, several cruise ships make Madeira a regular stop so that their passengers can sample and enjoy the quality hotels, restaurants, and shops found throughout the island.

The residents of the island have descended from many people, with English and Portuguese predominating. Although Portuguese is the principal language of most of the population, English is also common and both languages are used in business. Many of the residents are bilingual. The quality of life on Madeira is good, comparable to or better than the norms in Portugal. Excellent housing is available at reasonable prices, and visitors from the most advanced countries find in Madeira a modern infrastructure and telecommunications system.

Economy and Taxes

In hopes of expanding Madeira's economy and to improve the standard of living for their people, the Madeiran government in 1989 created the Madeira International Business Center (MIBC), whose purpose is to encourage and promote the region's business. The MIBC focuses on four major sectors:

- An offshore financial center, including banking, insurance, reinsurance, fund management, leasing, and other financial services.

- An industrial free trade zone, including all manufacturing and warehousing operations.

- International services, which includes various operations such as trading, holding, management, trusts, ship operations, and invoicing.

- An international ship register, including commercial vessels, oil rig platforms, and pleasure yachts.

In an effort to encourage investment, a variety of tax benefits are available to individuals and domestic and foreign companies.

- Specific incentives available to individuals include:

  - An exemption from income and withholding taxes on dividends, interest on loans of shareholders, and other types of income received by investors in companies that operate from within the free zone.

- An exemption from transfer, gift, and inheritance taxes in respect of all transfers of shares in the capital of companies that conduct their business from within the free zone.

• Incentives available to companies that operate in Madeira's free zone include:

- An exemption from taxes on income derived from business activity conducted in the zone until 2011.

- An exemption from local taxes.

- An exemption from municipal property taxes in regard to income derived from business activity in the free zone.

- An exemption from transfer, gift, and inheritance taxes on the acquisition of real estate for the purpose of establishing operations in the free zone.

- An exemption from taxes on capital gains generated from the sales of fixed assets.

- An exemption from having to withhold taxes from the payment of royalties.

- An exemption from having to withhold taxes from interest on loans from foreign banks and on bonds issued by companies, provided these funds are used for investment solely in the free zone.

- An exemption from VAT on imported goods, provided the goods are to be stored and/or transferred in the free zone.

- An exemption from custom duties on imported goods, provided the goods are to be stored and/or transferred in the free zone.

• Specific incentives are available to offshore financial services companies, including:

- An exemption from corporate taxes on all income obtained from operations conducted by the branch office, provided the operations are conducted wholly with non-residents in Portuguese territory or with other individuals or entities established in the free zone.

- An exemption from withholding taxes on revenues paid by branches in the funding of other business activities, provided the beneficiaries are non-residents in

Portuguese territories or are entities established in the free zone.

• Specific incentives are available to service companies whose business activities include trading, trusts, and similar operations. The following incentives apply:

> - An exemption from corporate taxes on income obtained from business activities until 2011, provided that such activities are conducted with entitles established within the Madeira International Business Center, or with non-residents in Portuguese territory.

> - An exemption from corporate taxes on the interest of loans. The contracted entities must be established within the Madeira International Business Center; also the loans must be used for operations within the MIBC and the lenders must be non-residents in Portuguese territory.

> - An exemption for non-resident shareholders in Portuguese territory from corporate and individual taxes in regard to dividends and income from interest and other forms of loans and advances of capital until 2011. The dividends must arise from the income of entities obtained from activities in the MIBC. This excludes

the proportion of non-exempt income from business activities conducted in Portuguese territory.

- Specific incentives are available to shipping companies through the International Shipping Registry of Madeira (MAR), including:

  - An exemption of tax on profits earned by companies which own ships under the Portuguese flag and transport cargo in international waters.

  - An exemption from taxes on dividends that are distributed to shareholders.

  - An exemption from duties on the inheritance of shares in a shipping company.

  - An exemption from capital gains tax which would be otherwise payable on the sale or transfer of a ship or shares in a shipping company.

  - An exemption from income tax on the salaries of the officers and crews of vessels operating in international waters.

Contact:

SDM – Sociedade de Desenvolvimento da Madeira
Edificio SDM, Rua da Mouraria 9, 1ˢᵗ Floor
9000 Funchal
Madeira
Tel: +351-291-201333
Fax: +351-291-201399

Embassy of Portugal
2125 Kalorama Rd., NW
Washington, D.C. 20008
Tel: 202-328-8610 or 202-328-9025
Fax: 202-462-3726

Consulate General of Portugal
630 Fifth Ave.
Suite 310-378
New York, NY 10111
Tel: 212-246-4580 or 212-765-2980
Fax: 212-459-0190

Consulate General of Portugal
3298 Washington St.
San Francisco, CA 94115
Tel: 415-921-1443
Fax: 415-346-1440

Malta

Near the center of the Mediterranean Sea, located between Italy and North Africa, Malta has served as a crossroads between continents for centuries. Malta is the largest island of a group of islands that includes Gozo, Comino, Cominotto, and Filfla. Together, the islands have an area of about 122 square miles (316 square kilometers); the island of Malta has an area of about 95 square miles (246 square kilometers).

Malta enjoys a delightful climate with temperatures averaging about 89° F (32° C) in the summer and 57° F (15° C) in the winter. Sunshine is plentiful.

About 370,000 people whose ancestry represents many of the lands around the Mediterranean and Europe live on Malta, enjoying a diverse and multi-faceted culture. English is the islands' official language, with Maltese and Italian also being widely spoken. The standard of living on Malta is among the best of Europe, quality health care is available to just about everyone, education is valued and free on all levels, and the infrastructure of the islands is fully modern.

Economy and Taxes

Malta has a diversified economy built around various industries, including textiles, high-tech products, machinery, food and beverages, and tourism. In recent years Malta has also grown in importance as an international financial services center. Numerous banks and financial services companies offer an astounding assortment of financial products and services.

With a goal of promoting investment in Malta and sustaining the islands' economy, the government has included various tax exemptions and incentives aimed at both individuals and companies. Following are incentives for individuals:

- There are no property taxes, real estate taxes, local, or municipal taxes in Malta.

- Income arising outside of Malta, including capital gains, are subject to tax only if the recipient is both domiciled and a resident of Malta.

- Expatriates are not required to pay tax on capital gains.

- Foreign residents are taxed only a small percentage on the amount they bring into the country for living expenses.

The following incentives are designed for businesses

- Companies which are at least 95% export-oriented may   receive a tax holiday of ten years.

- Companies may be eligible for special investment tax credits.

- Specific companies may be eligible for an accelerated allowance for depreciation.

- Specific companies may be eligible for reduced rates for reinvested profits.

- Specific companies may be eligible for duty-free importation of parts or materials.

- Specific companies may be eligible for duty-free shipment of various products shipped to EC countries.

- Specific companies may be eligible for reduced tariffs on products exported to the U.S.

Contact:

Malta National Tourist Office
Empire State Building
350 Fifth Ave.
Suite 4412
New York, NY 10118
Tel: 212-695-9520
Fax: 212-695-8229

Malta Tourist Office
280 Republic St.
Valletta CMR 02
Malta
Tel: 22-44-44/5 or 22-50-48/9
Fax: 22-04-01

The Embassy of Malta
2017 Connecticut Ave., NW
Washington, D.C. 20008
Tel: 202-462-3611/2
Fax: 202-387-5470

The Malta Development Corporation
P.O. Box 141
Marsa GPO 01
Malta
Tel: +356-667-100
Fax: +356-667-111

Monaco

Located in southeastern France, Monaco is a small independent principality with an area of slightly less than a square mile. Best known as a resort of the rich, the enclave is in fact affordable for investors of modest means. Surrounded by France except on the south where the Mediterranean touches its shores, Monaco possesses a climate with few extremes. Mild winters and warm summers with plenty of sunshine through the year make the enclave a delightful place. Monaco is a wealthy enclave that offers its residents one of the finest lifestyles in the world.

Some 30,000 people reside in Monaco. About 12,000 of the enclave's residents are French, 5,000 are Italian, 5,000 are Monegasques, with the remainder comprised of other Europeans. Monaco's official language is French, however, many of the residents speak Monegasque, a mixture of French and Italian. English is also common.

Economy and Taxes

Several sectors provide the foundation of Monaco's economy, including tourism, banking and insurance, and the production of electronic equipment, pharmaceuticals, and cosmetics. The gambling casino at Monte Carlo also is a major source of government revenue. Some of the world's largest banks, including American Express, Citibank, Chase, Credit Suisse, Grindlays, and NatWest, are represented in Monaco. The government offers various tax incentives:

- Monaco has no personal income tax. French nationals under specific conditions are excluded, however.

- The Monegasque fund, a special fund created in Monaco, is not subject to income tax or capital gains tax in the enclave. Also, investors in the fund are not subject to income tax or capital gains tax from the fund's proceeds in Monaco.

- Closely-held investment trusts enjoy locally tax-free administration.

Contact:

The Monaco Government Tourist and Convention Bureau
565 Fifth Ave.
New York, NY 10017
Tel: 212-286-3330 or 800-753-9696
Fax: 212-286-9890

Monaco Tourist Board and Convention Bureau
2A, Boulevard des Moulins
Monte Carlo, MC 98000
Monaco
Tel: 377-92-166116
Fax: 377-92-166000

Panama

Positioned at the southernmost part of North America, Panama links the North with South America. The republic is also home to the Panama Canal, which it officially took control of from the United States at the end of 1999. A long, narrow country, highlighted with rugged interior mountains, Panama has an area of 29,762 square miles (77,082 square kilometers). It has easy access to both the Atlantic and Pacific Oceans, as well as the two continents through Costa Rica to the north and Colombia to the south. Panama is one of the prime crossroads of the world.

Panama has a tropical climate in which heat and humidity predominate. Average annual temperatures along the coasts range from 73° F to 81° F (23° to 27° C), with temperatures cooling slightly as elevation increases. Although a drier season prevails from January to May, rainfall is somewhat high throughout the year, with the east coast receiving more rain than the west.

About 2.7 million people live in Panama. Mestizos make up the majority of the population, with whites accounting for about 10%, West Indians 14%, and Indians 6%. Spanish is the official language, but many people, particularly the educated, speak English as well. The standard of living in Panama on average is better than that of most Latin American countries. The country's infrastructure, especially in Panama City, the capital, and in and around the Canal Zone, is modern and efficient.

Economy and Taxes

Panama's economy is founded on commerce, banking and financial services, and tourism. In recent years the country has gained prominence as an international financial center. Although tax rates on local income are high in Panama, the country's tax code provides a variety of significant incentives, including:

- Income from foreign sources is not subject to tax.

- Projects and enterprises that fall within the tourism sector are eligible for numerous incentives, including:

  - An exemption from taxes on assets.

  - An exemption from taxes on capital.

  - Up to a 20 years' exemption on real estate taxes.

  - An exemption from income tax on the interest earned by creditors conducting business that invests in hotels.

  - An exemption from income tax for 15 years if the project is located in one of nine geographical zones designated for tourist development.

115

- A reduction of 50% of taxable income is possible for individuals and companies who invest in stocks or bonds issued by tourist companies.

Contact:

Panama Consulate of New York
1212 Avenue of the Americas
10th Floor
New York, NY 10036
Tel: 212-840-2450
Fax: 212-840-2469

Panama Consulate of Washington, D.C.
2862 McGill Terrace, NW
Washington, D.C. 20008
Tel: 202-483-1407
Fax: 202-387-6141

Panama Consulate of Miami
444 Brickell Ave.
Suite 729
Miami, FL 33131
Tel: 305-371-7031
Fax: 305-371-2907

Panama Consulate of Los Angeles
435 North Roxbury Drive
Suite 207
Beverly Hills, CA 90210
Tel: 310-859-7583
Fax: 310-273-5339

The Panama Tourist Bureau
P.O. Box 4421, Zone 5
The Republic of Panama
Tel: +507-226-7000 or +507-226-3544
Fax: +507-226-3483 or +507-226-6856

Portugal

Lying amidst the trade routes that connect northern and southern Europe, Africa, North and South America, and Asia, Portugal enjoys a prime location in the western part of the Iberian Peninsula for it. Portugal's area, including the islands of Madeira and the Azores, is 35,553 square miles (92,082 square kilometers). The country possesses a varying topography between coastal plains and interior mountains.

Portugal's climate varies with latitude and elevation, being mostly temperate in the north and Mediterranean in the southern lowlands. Average annual temperatures range from about 50° F (10° C) in the north to around 68° F (20° C) in the south. Winters are generally mild and of short duration. The country's overall rainfall is somewhat low, with the north receiving more rain than the south.

Portugal has a population of about 10 million with most of its people able to trace their ancestry to Iberians and Moors. Portuguese, of course, is the principal language, however, many people, particularly the educated, speak English. French is common in some of the country's northern regions. Portugal's standard of living compares favorably with the levels common throughout most of Europe. While the country's infrastructure is adequate, the government has committed some $20 billion in recent years to modernize transportation and communications systems.

Economy and Taxes

Portugal's economy has been one of Europe's leaders over the last several years. The country has also become an attractive site for investment. Between the years 1986 and 1992, for example, direct foreign investment increased from $164 million to $4.4 billion. Investment has continued at impressive rates throughout the nineties. Portugal joined the European Union (EU) in 1986 and since then the government has established programs to open Portugal to world trade, promote business, and encourage investment. In may of 1998 Portugal became a member of the European Monetary Union (EMU), further enhancing its position in trade.

118

To encourage investment a variety of tax incentives are available to specific types of business, including:

- Real estate holding companies that were incorporated during or after 1989 may be entitled to a reduced corporate tax rate of 25% for a period of between seven and ten years.

- Only 50% of the dividends on shares obtained during a process of privatization are subject to tax for a period of five years after the date of acquisition.

- Companies that undertake major investment projects aimed at increasing exports may be eligible for tax incentives formulated on an individual basis.

Additional incentives are available in Madeira, which is a part of Portugal and which offers its own incentives to encourage investment. Refer to the section on Madeira previously in this text.

Contact:

Embassy of Portugal
2125 Kalorama Rd., NW
Washington, D.C. 20008
Tel: 202-328-8610 or 202-328-9025
Fax: 202-462-3726

Consulate General of Portugal
630 Fifth Ave.
Suite 310-378
New York, NY 10111
Tel: 212-246-4580 or 212-765-2980
Fax: 212-459—0190

Consulate General of Portugal
3298 Washington St.
San Francisco, CA 94115
Tel: 415-921-1443
Fax: 415-346-1440

Portuguese Trade Commission
590 Fifth Ave., 3rd Floor
New York, NY 10036-4702
Tel: 212-345-4610
Fax: 212-575-4737

Portuguese National Tourist Office
590 Fifth Ave., 4th Floor
New York, NY 10036-4704
Tel: 212-354-4403
Fax: 212-764-6137

Portuguese Trade and Tourism Office
1900 L St., NW
Suite 310
Washington, D.C. 20036
Tel: 202-331-8222
Fax: 202-331-8236

Portuguese Trade and Tourism Office
88 Kearny St.
Suite 1770
San Francisco, CA 941-8
Tel: 415-391-7080
Fax: 415-391-7147

Puerto Rico

Puerto Rico is the largest island of an island group located about 950 miles (about 1600 kilometers) southeast of Miami. The official name of the group is the Commonwealth of Puerto Rico; it is a territory of the United States but it enjoys internal self-government.

The island of Puerto Rico is a rough rectangle with an area of about 3,500 square miles (9,100 square kilometers). Coastal lowlands rise into hills and a mountainous interior that in some places has an elevation of more than 4,000 feet (about 1,300 meters). The trade winds blowing from the east bring plentiful rainfall and much of the island is covered with tropical rainforests. Temperatures vary little and remain warm throughout the year. Even in the highlands temperatures are relatively constant and not much cooler than the coasts.

Close to four million people live in Puerto Rico with about 1.5 million living in San Juan, the capital. Puerto Rico's population is a mix of Spanish, other Europeans, Africans, and Native Americans. Together its people have created a unique and fascinating culture. Spanish and English are official languages, however, Spanish is the first language for most Puerto Ricans. Spanish is also the language of business.

Puerto Rico has one of the finest standards of living in Latin America. The island infrastructure is of high quality, and its telecommunication systems are state-of-the-art.

Economy and Taxes

Puerto Rico's economy is one of the strongest and most diverse of all the Caribbean. Its economy typically outperforms those of its neighbors, and the Puerto Rican people have the third highest per capita income in the Western Hemisphere, surpassed only by the United States and Canada. Of all Latin American nations, only Mexico and Brazil exceed Puerto Rico's total volume in external trade. Since 1993, the island's annual GDP has averaged 7%; in 1996 the GDP was $45.5 billion.

The island's prosperity is a direct result of far-sighted government initiatives begun in the late 1940s. Realizing that the island's economy needed to be diversified if it was to expand and remain competitive, the island government established the Economic Development Agency (EDA) in 1950, its objective being to assist local and mainland investors in their efforts to establish manufacturing operations on the island. Various incentives, including tax benefits, were offered to encourage investment. Today, Puerto Rico's economic engine is fueled by manufacturing, tourism, and a vigorous service sector. Puerto Rico has also become a regional financial services center, with many major banks from the U.S., Canada, and Spain, as well as numerous financial services companies, represented on the island. It has been estimated that close to $40 billion is controlled by Puerto Rican financial services firms and banks.

Puerto Rico's tax system offers a variety of incentives, including:

- Residents of Puerto Rico do not pay federal income taxes, except in cases in which they derive income from sources outside the island.

- Corporate profits earned in Puerto Rico receive federal tax credits after the profits are remitted to U.S. parent companies.

- Companies whose operations focus on manufacturing are eligible for an exemption of 90% from Puerto Rico taxes, including state taxes on corporate earnings, real estate, and personal property. These exemptions may last for a period of 10 to 25 years, depending upon the location of the company.

- Service companies are eligible for an exemption of 90% from Puerto Rico taxes, including state taxes on corporate earnings, real estate, and personal property. These exemptions may last for a period of 10 to 25 years, depending upon the location of the company.

- Companies may be eligible for an exemption of 60% on excise and other taxes required for licenses throughout the time of the tax exemption.

- Companies may defer their tax-exempt years on an annual basis.

- Companies whose operations include special projects in tourism may be eligible for specific incentives as a result of the Tourism Development Law of 1993, including:

  - Approved projects may receive an exemption from various taxes for a 10-year period. The exemptions may be renewed for another period of up to 10 years.

124

- Income and dividends from tourism projects may be exempt from taxes at a rate of up to 90%. In the islands of Vieques and Culebra, the exemption may be 100%.

- Approved projects may be eligible for a 50% tax credit in regard to investments.

• Companies operating in Puerto Rico's free trade zones enjoy specific incentives, including:

- An exemption for export manufacturing.

- A tax-free and duty-free base that lies within the jurisdiction of the United States.

In addition, the 1998 Tax Incentives Act provides many enhanced deductions and inducements, including:

• Companies new to Puerto Rico or companies already established on the island and planning to expand their operations by at least 25% may be eligible for the following:

- A minimum-maximum income tax of 2% to 7%.

- A 200% deduction for research and development.

- A full expenses deduction for investment in buildings, machinery, or equipment in the same year.

- A 200% deduction for job training costs.

- Elimination of the "Tollgate" tax, which is a tax at the time of distribution on dividends repatriated to the parent company.

- A total exemption from real and personal property taxes during initial construction during the first year of operation and 90% thereafter.

- Qualified companies are not subject to tax on passive income derived from eligible investments made from industrial development income.

- Manufacturers may be eligible for a 100% exemption from excise taxes on raw materials, machinery and equipment, and in some cases excise taxes on fuels.

- An exemption from income tax on interest earned by financial institutions on loans up to $50,000 to small- and medium-sized companies for the purpose of expansion.

Contact:

The Puerto Rico Development Administration
666 Fifth Ave., 15th Floor
New York, NY 10103
Tel: 1-888-5-PRIDCO

The Puerto Rico Economic Development Administration
233 N. Michigan Ave.
Chicago, IL 60601
Tel: 312-565-0910

The Puerto Rico Economic Development Administration
355 F.D. Roosevelt Ave.
Hato Rey
Puerto Rico 00918
Tel: 1-888-5-PRIDCO

The Puerto Rico Chamber of Commerce
P.O. Box 9024033
San Juan, PR 00902-4033
Tel: 787-721-6060
Fax: 787-723-1891

The Puerto Rico Tourism Company
666 Fifth Ave., 15th Floor
New York, NY 10103
Tel: 1-800-866-STAR

The Puerto Rico Tourism Company
901 Ponce de Leon Blvd.
Suite 101
Coral Gables, FL 33134
Tel: 1-800-866-STAR

St. Kitts and Nevis

St. Kitts and Nevis comprise a two-island nation in the Caribbean Sea about one-third of the way from Puerto Rico to Trinidad and Tobago. Together, the islands have an area of about 102 square miles (about 269 square kilometers). The islands possess a subtropical climate in which there is little seasonal variation of temperature, which hovers around 80° F (27° C), however, rainfall varies with a rainy season occurring between May and November.

Slightly more than 40,000 people live on St. Kitts and Nevis, most being descended from Africans. The islands have a long association with Great Britain, and British influence is apparent. English is the principal language and British architecture and traditions are common. St. Kitts and Nevis have a solid infrastructure and offer a high quality of life.

Economy and Taxes

The economy of St. Kitts and Nevis center around tourism, light manufacturing, agriculture, and a vibrant financial services sector that increasingly has played a greater role in the islands' prosperity.

Although St. Kitts and Nevis created the only International Financial Center in the Caribbean in April of 1997, the financial services sector has grown rapidly. The banks and companies that comprise the sector complement the offshore trust services centered on Nevis.

When the Island Assembly of Nevis adopted the Nevis International Trust Ordinance in 1994, it created one of the most flexible and comprehensive asset protection trust (APT) laws in the world. The Nevis APT rapidly gained popularity among international investors because of the excellent protection it provides. A Nevis trust places personal assets out of the reach of foreign governments and their agencies, creditors, litigious plaintiffs, and lawyers. The law is quite clear in its application. Nevis judges will not recognize any non-domestic court orders regarding any APT established in Nevis. Any foreign creditor or agency must try its suit through the courts of Nevis, regardless of any previous legal actions or judgments. In addition, anyone bringing a suit against an APT established in Nevis must first post a bond of U.S.$25,000 with the government to be applied as necessary to court and other costs. Further, the statute of limitations for filing a legal challenge to an APT established in Nevis runs out a year from the date of the creation of the trust. On top of all this, the burden of proof is carried by the foreign claimant, especially in cases where fraudulent intent of the trust or on the part of its officers or beneficiaries is claimed.

Along with its asset protection, Nevis APTs permit the same individual to serve as creator, beneficiary, and protector of the trust. This goes well beyond the trust laws of most jurisdictions, and gives an individual significant control over his assets.

APTs also provide privacy. Trust documents are not required to be filed with the Nevisian government and thus do not appear in the public record, assuring confidentiality. The only information required to established an APT on Nevis is a simple document identifying the trustee, the date the trust is established, the date of filing, and the name of the local trust company that represents the APT. A filing fee of U.S.$200 is necessary, as is an annual fee of U.S.$200 for maintenance.

In addition to the benefits of APTs on Nevis, St. Kitts and Nevis also offer major tax incentives, including:

- There are no personal income taxes in St. Kitts and Nevis.

- The islands have no sales taxes.

- The islands have no gift taxes.

- The islands have no estate duties.

- Corporate tax holidays from 10 to 15 years are available for eligible companies.

- Companies that produce goods exclusively for export outside the CARICOM region may be eligible for a tax holiday up to 15 years. (Upon conclusion of the tax holiday, a further tax concession in the form of a rebate of a portion of the income tax paid, based on export profits as a percentage of total profits, may be available. This rebate may range from 25% to 50%.

- Companies may be eligible for an exemption from import duties on raw materials, parts, and production supplies.

- Owners of hotels of more than 30 bedrooms may be exempt from income tax for a period of 10 years. Owners of hotels of less than 30 bedrooms may qualify for an exemption of tax on profits for five years.

Contact:

Consulate of St. Kitts and Nevis
Economic Affairs Division
414 E. 75th St.
New York, NY 10021
Tel: 212-535-1234
Fax: 212-535-6854

Ministry of Trade and Industry
P.O. Box 600
Church St.
Basseterre, St. Kitts
West Indies
Tel: +1-869-465-2302
Fax: +1-869-465-1778

The Embassy of St. Kitts and Nevis
3216 New Mexico Ave., NW
Washington, D.C. 20016
Tel: 202-686-2636
Fax: 202-686-5740

Department of Tourism, St. Kitts and Nevis
Pelican Mall, Bay Rd.
P.O. Box 132
Basseterre, St. Kitts
West Indies
Tel: +1-869-465-2620/4040
Fax: +1-869-465-8794

Nevis Tourism Bureau
Main St.
Charlestown, Nevis
West Indies
Tel: +1-869-469-1042
Fax: +1-869-469-1066

St. Kitts and Nevis Tourism Office
365 Bay St.
Suite 806
Toronto, Ontario M5H 2V1
Canada
Tel: 416-368-6707
Fax: 416-368-3934

Turks and Caicos

The Turks and Caicos are two island groups southeast of the Bahamas. The Turks consist of Grand Turk, Salt Cay and several uninhabited cays, while the Caicos include Grand Caicos and five other islands. The overall area of the islands is about 165 square miles (430 square kilometers). The Turks and Caicos enjoy a tropical marine climate with abundant sunshine, and average annual temperatures of about 85° F (29° C).

About 14,500 people live on the islands. The island groups are British dependencies, and although most of the residents are of African or mixed descent, English is the official language and British influence is pronounced. The British have maintained a modern infrastructure and telecommunications system, and the standard of living on the islands is of high quality.

Economy and Taxes

Tourism and offshore financial services are the principal sectors of the islands' economy. In a program to encourage investment, the government offers numerous tax incentives, including:

- There is no income tax on the islands.

- There is no tax on capital gains.

- There is no tax on corporate dividends.

- There is not withholding tax.

- There is no tax on property.

- There is no value added tax.

- There is no sales tax.

- There are no taxes on estates, inheritances, gifts, or successions.

- There are no exchange controls.

Contact:

TCIvest
Chief Executive Officer
Hibiscus Square, Pond St.
P.O. Box 105
Grand Turk
Tel: 649-94-62058/2852
Fax: 649-94-61464

Turks and Caicos Islands Tourist Board
11645 Biscayne Blvd.
Suite 302
North Miami, FL 33181
Tel: 305-891-4117 or 800-241-0824
Fax: 305-891-7096

The United Kingdom

The United Kingdom, commonly called Great Britain or simply England, includes the island of Great Britain (shared by England, Scotland, and Wales), and the northern one-sixth of the island of Ireland. The overall area of the United

Kingdom is 94,227 square miles (244,046 square kilometers). The topography of Great Britain consists mostly of rugged hills and low mountains in the north and plains in east and southeast.

The islands of England and Ireland have temperate climates with milder temperatures than one would expect at their latitude. Average annual temperatures range between 52° F (about 11° C) in the south and 48° F (about 9° C) in the north. Few extremes in temperatures are the norm. With winds typically blowing in from the Atlantic, fog, mist, and clouds are more common than sunshine.

The population of the United Kingdom is about 58.5 million. More than 80% of the people are English with Scots, Irish, Welsh, and various other minority groups comprising the remainder. The people of the United Kingdom enjoy a fully modern infrastructure and excellent standard of living.

Economy and Taxes

The United Kingdom is one of the world's great commercial and financial centers. Its diversified economy is the fourth largest of Western Europe.

Although the United Kingdom does not offer tax incentives as many tax havens do, within the British tax code is the phrase "resident but not domiciled." The phrase bestows special tax status under specific conditions. What it means is that an individual can live in England and therefore be a resident, but not be domiciled there, meaning that he does not maintain his or permanent home in Great Britain. Such individuals can maintain a permanent home in another country but reside, or live, in Britain. Individuals who are "resident but not domiciled" are required to pay tax only on income that is actually brought into the United Kingdom. Consequently, an individual can accumulate income earned abroad in offshore accounts and not be taxed on these funds under British tax law.

A note of caution is necessary here. Because the strategy is somewhat complex, individuals considering taking advantage of the "resident but not domiciled" provision are advised to consult the services of a tax advisor experienced with British tax law, particularly in regard to the residency issue.

Contact:

The British Consulate
845 Third Ave.
New York, NY 10022

Tel: 212-745-0200 or 212-745-0495
Fax: 212-745-3062 or 212-745-0456

The British Consulate
Federal Reserve Plaza
25th Floor
600 Atlantic Ave.
Boston, MA 02210
Tel: 617-248-9555
Fax: 617-248-9578

The British Consulate
13th Floor
The Wrigley Building
400 N. Michigan Ave.
Chicago, IL 60611
Tel: 312-346-1810
Fax: 312-464-0661

The British Consulate
Suite 2700, 27th Floor
Marquis 1 Tower
245 Peachtree Center Ave.
Atlanta, GA 30303
Tel: 404-524-5856
Fax: 404-524-3153

The British Consulate
11766 Wilshire Blvd.
Suite 400
Los Angeles, CA 90025
Tel: 310-477-3322

The Republic of Ireland

The Republic of Ireland should not be confused with Northern Ireland. Although the two share the island of Ireland, the Republic of Ireland is an independent nation while Northern Ireland remains a part of Great Britain. Because of the on-going tensions between Protestants and Catholics, Northern Ireland garners much of the world's news headlines, overshadowing the Republic of Ireland that has quietly emerged as a haven of investment and tax incentives.

The Republic of Ireland covers the greater part of the island of Ireland with an area of about 27,000 square miles (about 70 square kilometers). Northern Ireland has an area of about 5,500 square miles (10,110 square kilometers). The coast varies, being relatively flat in the east and characterized by islets and steep cliffs in the west. The climate of the island is about 25° F (14° C) warmer than one would expect to find at its northern position because of the effects of the Gulf Stream, a mild ocean current that washes over the island's shores. Originating in the tropical waters south of the United States, then flowing along the eastern coast and then across the North Atlantic to Europe, the Gulf Stream warms the atmosphere above it, moderating Ireland's temperatures. The island's average summer temperatures range between 57° and

68° F (about 14° to 20° C) with winter temperatures averaging between 40° and 45° F (about 7° to 14° C).

About 3.7 million people live in the Republic of Ireland, with about one-third living in and around Dublin, the capital and largest city. Most of the population has descended from the Celts, an ancient group of people thought to have originated in Europe and spread throughout the continent and British Isles. An English minority is also present. English and Irish (Gaelic) are the country's official languages. English is most commonly spoken. The standard of living in the Republic of Ireland is comparable to most of the other countries that belong to the European Union, and the country's infrastructure and telecommunications systems are modern and advanced. The Republic of Ireland is a beautiful nation, considered by many to be one of the most pollution-free countries of Europe, if not the world.

Economy and Taxes

The government of the Irish Republic has taken various steps over the last several years to promote the country's economy. Policies to promote the growth of light industry, tourism, and the financial sector have centered around substantial tax incentives, available to both residents and for-

eigners. The following facts demonstrate the overall strength
of the Irish Republic's economy:

- The Republic of Ireland has only about 1% of the
  European Union's population, but attracts nearly
  25% of U.S. investment in manufacturing in
  Europe.

- Over the last 20 years, 40% of inward investment
  in the electronics sector of Europe has been
  targeted for Ireland.

- Of the ten largest software companies in the world,
  five have development or production facilities in
  Ireland, which produces close to 60% of all the
  software sold in Europe.

- Of the world's top 15 pharmaceutical companies,
  13 maintain research and development and/or
  production facilities on the island.

- The Dublin International Financial Services
  Center has emerged as the favored location within
  the EU for the financial services industry.

Truly impressive growth has occurred in the country's
financial services sector over the past ten to fifteen years.
Indeed, the Irish Republic has become a leading financial
services center, with Dublin being recognized as a major
center for international offshore funds management in Europe.
The nation's financial services sector includes various banks,

investment and funds companies, credit companies, and credit unions. The many companies of this sector offer investors numerous services, including international banking, funds management, asset finance, and insurance.

A cursory look at the tax code of the Republic of Ireland reveals that the country charges various taxes, including income tax. A closer look, however, makes it clear that major tax incentives are provided.

- Foreign income (except income from the United Kingdom) is not taxable for non-domiciled residents, unless the income is remitted to Ireland.

- Non-residents are not subject to withholding tax on interest payments they receive from a financial services company located at the Customs House Docks Area in Dublin.

- Manufacturing companies may be eligible for a 10% corporate tax rate. (The normal rate is 40%). For qualifying companies, the 10% rate is available until the year 2010.

- International financial services companies located in Dublin may be eligible for a 10% tax rate on profits derived from certified activities. In addition they may be eligible for a 10-year exemption on local property taxes, a 100% write-off for expenditures for new equipment during the first year of operation, a 100% write-off for the costs of new facilities in the first year for owners who occupy their sites, and a 54% write-off for new building costs in the first year for lessors. Companies may also be eligible to enjoy freedom of withholding tax in the payment of interest to recipients.

• Companies granted permission to conduct their operations in the Shannon Airport Customs Free Zone may be eligible for a tax rate of 10% through December of 2005.

Contact:

The Irish Industrial Development Authority
17th Floor
345 Park Ave.
New York, NY 10154
Tel: 212-750-4300
Fax: 212-750-7357

The Irish Industrial Development Authority
The Statler Building
20 Park Plaza
Suite 520
Boston, MA 02116
Tel: 617-484-8225
Fax: 617-338-4745

The Irish Industrial Development Authority
P.O. Box 190129
Atlanta, GA 31119-0129
Tel: 770-351-8474
Fax: 770-351-8568

The Irish Industrial Development Authority
75 E. Wacker Drive
Suite 600
Chicago, IL 60601-3708
Tel: 312-236-0222
Fax: 312-236-3407

The Irish Industrial Development Authority
1620 26th St.
Suite 480 South
Santa Monica, CA 90404
Tel: 310-829-0081
Fax: 310-829-1586

The Irish Industrial Development Authority
Wilton Park House
Wilton Place
Dublin 2
Ireland
Tel: 00-353-0-1-603-4000
Fax: 00-353-0-1-603-4040

The Irish Tourist Board
345 Park Ave.
New York, NY 10154
Tel: 212-418-0800 or 800-223-6470
Fax: 212-371-9052

The Irish Tourist Board
Baggot Street Bridge
Dublin 8
Ireland

Tel: +353-1-602-4000
Fax: +353-1-602-4000

The Irish Embassy in the U.S.
2234 Massachusetts Ave., NW
Washington, D.C. 20008
Tel: 202-462-3939 or 202-462-3940
Fax: 202-232-5993

Tax Havens of the East

The tax havens of the East begin with states in the Middle East and include countries and jurisdictions of Asia and the Pacific. While most Americans are more familiar with the Caribbean, South America, or Europe, and may be more likely to consider tax havens in these places, some of the tax havens in the East offer truly impressive incentives. Moreover, after the recession the east suffered through during the last years of the nineties, it is likely that the economies of many Asian and Pacific nations will rebound strongly, resulting in superior investment opportunities. Following are some of the best tax havens of the East.

Dubai

Dubai is one of the seven, oil-rich states of the United Arab Emirates located along the southern coast of the Persian Gulf. The state is small and its land is mostly barren; most of Dubai is desert.

Like many of the lands of the Middle East, Dubai receives only a few inches of rainfall per year. Summers are hot and winters are mild.

Slightly over a half million people live in Dubai. Most are of Arab descent, however foreigners who work for the state comprise a rather large percentage. Foreign workers come from many countries, with the greatest numbers coming from Iran, Europe, and India. Although Arabic is the state's official language, English is widely spoken and both Arabic and English are common in business. The standard of living in Dubai is excellent, due primarily to oil wealth. Recognizing the importance of foreign professionals and workers to its economy, the government of Dubai has made provisions to make their stay in the state comfortable and enjoyable.

Economy and Taxes

Dubai's high quality of life is a result of the oil industry. However, the state's leaders, aware that the oil beneath the desert sands is expected to last only another 30 years at present rates of consumption, have embarked upon a program of economic diversification. With the establishment of the Jebel Ali Free Zone and a modern infrastructure, the state's leaders hope to turn Dubai into a regional center for industry and trade.

Along with creating a pro-business atmosphere, they have also provided for numerous incentives for businesses in the Jebel Ali Free Zone. The incentives are available to domestic companies as well as those owned entirely by foreigners. The incentives include:

- An exemption from corporate taxes for at least 15 years. This initial 15-year period may be renewed for an additional 15 years.

- An exemption of personal taxes for at least 15 years. This initial 15-year period is renewable for another 15 years.

- An exemption from import and export duties payable within the free zone.

In addition, companies established in the free zone enjoy no barriers or restrictions on imports, no foreign exchange controls, and minimal bureaucracy. There are no restrictions of currency in the free zone.

Contact:

The Dubai Department of Tourism and Marketing
8 Penn Center, 19th Floor
Philadelphia, PA 19103
Tel: 215-751-9750
Fax: 215-751-9551

The Dubai Department of Tourism and Marketing
901 Wilshire Blvd.
Santa Monica, CA 90401
Tel: 310-752-4488
Fax: 310-752-4444

Guam

The U.S. territory of Guam is southernmost of the Mariana Islands. Located about 6,000 miles west of Hawaii, 1,500 miles southeast of Tokyo, 1,500 miles east of Manila, and 2,100 miles east-southeast of Hong Kong, it occupies a prime position as a gateway to the Orient. The island government's commitment to economic diversification and growth through a variety of tax incentives makes it a fine potential site for investment as well.

Having an area of 209 square miles (540 square kilometers), Guam is the largest of the Marianas. The island possesses a tropical climate with pleasant average annual temperatures of about 80° F (27° C).

Some 130,000 people are residents of the island. About 20,000 of the population are U.S. military personnel and their dependents who are stationed on Guam, which is a major

Pacific defense site. The rest of the population is comprised mostly of Micronesians. English and Chamorro — the traditional language of Micronesia – are the principal languages of the island, however, English predominates in government, business, and education. The infrastructure, telecommunications, and standard of living on Guam are good, all benefitting from U.S. presence and support. Guam may lack the exciting, bustling atmosphere of some of the Caribbean islands, but it offers an enjoyable lifestyle and exceptional environment.

Economy and Taxes

Capitalizing on its strategic position for trade in the Pacific, Guam's economy has expanded and diversified in recent years. The following sectors offer excellent potential: agriculture, aquaculture, construction, financial services, manufacturing, wholesaling, and retailing. Shipping is important, too. Apra Harbor, Guam's commercial port, is the largest deep-water port between Hawaii and Asia. It is designed to handle commerce, and it is considered by many to be one of the most efficient seaports in the world.

In an effort to foster the island's economy, the government of Guam, through the Guam Economic Development

Authority, offers tax incentives to qualified investors. The incentives are based on investment commitment and the potential for creating new jobs with the primary objective being to expand the island's economy. While various companies can benefit from the incentives, the incentives are designed primarily for companies whose operations focus on one or more of the following: manufacturing, insurance, high technology, agriculture, specialized medical facilities, and fishing. Qualified companies may be granted several incentives, including:

- A 100% income tax rebate for up to 20 years.

- A 100% abatement on real property for up to 10 years.

- A 75% rebate on corporate dividends for up to five years.

- An abatement on gross receipts tax on petroleum and alcoholic beverages made in Guam for up to 10 years.

- Firms licensed to do business on Guam are exempt from U.S. federal income taxes, however, they are required to pay a territorial tax.

- Interest earned through the operation of an offshore lender is not treated as a Guam source income.

Contact:

The Guam Economic Development Authority
ITC Building
Suite 511
590 So. Marine Dr.
Tamuning, Guam 96911
Tel: 671-647-4332/4141
Fax: 671-649-4146

Department of Revenue and Taxation
Government of Guam
Building 13-1
Mariner Ave.
Tiyan
Barrigada, Guam 96913
Tel: 671-475-5000
Fax: 671-472-2643

Hong Kong

When Hong Kong, officially the Hong Kong Special Administrative Region (Hong Kong SAR), was reunited with China on July 1, 1997, many people were worried that Hong Kong's robust economy and pro-business climate would deteriorate. This has not been the case. Today most people living and working in Hong Kong believe that the city will continue to be a center for business and investment opportunities for many years.

Located in eastern Asia on the South China Sea, Hong Kong consists of a part of the mainland and several islands. Overall, the area of Hong Kong SAR is 403 square miles (1,045 square kilometers). Its climate is warm in summer, mild in fall and spring, and a bit cooler in winter, though there are few extremes in temperature. Spring and summer are somewhat wetter than fall and winter, however, on the whole the region receives ample sunshine and pleasant weather.

Hong Kong's population is about 6.3 million, of which close to 90% are Chinese. The remaining 10% of its residents include people from around the world. Principal languages are Cantonese (Chinese) and English, which is often used in international business. Hong Kong's infrastructure and telecommunications are of high quality and its standard of living is one of the highest in the world.

Economy and Taxes

Hong Kong's GDP of U.S. $27,500 ranks among the world's highest. Its free market system is one of the most open and the investment opportunities it offers are some of the best that can be found anywhere.

Hong Kong is one of the few jurisdictions in the world that can be described as both a business and tax haven. In most tax havens, a variety of financial services are offered, but there is usually little opportunity to add value to the services. Trading companies, for example, do little more than reinvoicing in the typical tax haven. In Hong Kong, however, the idea of a tax haven has been expanded to turn Hong Kong into an offshore business center.

ICS Trust Company Limited (a part of the ICS International group of companies) is a good example here. ICS, with its staff of 40 highly qualified professionals, offers services that apply to all operations of a business, including incorporation, financing, management, and investment of profits. Counted among ICS's clients are multinational companies as well as international investors who are interested in estate planning and tax shelters.

The woman behind ICS is Elizabeth L. Thomson, who describes herself as "a lawyer by profession" and "an entrepreneur by choice." She has helped people around the world to start successful businesses, and has especially helped many women entrepreneurs in Hong Kong.

ICS can help any business or investor enter or expand into Asian markets. ICS has the expertise and contacts to help clients arrange financing, secure the services of factories, shipping firms, and freight carriers, and also help in facilities and operations. It can help you to operate your business or investments effectively and efficiently.

If you would like to learn more about ICS and how they can help you with your business or investment goals, contact them at:

> ICS Trust (Asia) Limited
> 2700 Vicwood Plaza
> 199 Des Voeus Road, Central
> Hong Kong
> Tel: +852-2854-4544
> Fax: +852-2543-5555

In addition to its pro-business climate, Hong Kong also offers major tax incentives to investors, including:

- Only income derived from Hong Kong is taxable.

- Companies are required to pay only a 16% corporate tax, which is among the lowest in the region.

- There is no value added tax.

- There is no sales tax.

- There is no capital gains tax.

- There is no withholding tax on dividends and interest.

- There is a commissionary corporate tax of only 8% for offshore business of professional reinsurance firms authorized in Hong Kong.

- Generous tax deductions are available for research and development.

- A 100% write-off for new expenditures on plants and machinery specifically related to manufacturing, computer hardware, and software is available.

- An initial allowance of 20% on capital expenditures incurred in the construction of industrial buildings and other structures is available.

Contact:

Hong Kong Economic and Trade Office
115 East 54th St.
New York, NY 10022

Tel: 212-752-3320
Fax: 212-752-3395

Hong Kong Economic and Trade Office
1520 18ᵗʰ St., NW
Washington, D.C. 20036
Tel: 202-331-8947
Fax: 202-331-8958

Hong Kong Economic and Trade Office
130 Montgomery St.
San Francisco, CA 94104
Tel: 415-835-9300
Fax: 415-421-0646

Hong Kong Economic and Trade Office
174 St. George St.
Toronto, Ontario M5R 2M7
Canada
Tel: 416-924-5544
Fax: 416-924-3599

Jordan

Surrounded by Syria, Iraq, Saudi Arabia, and Israel, Jordan is a Middle East nation with an enviable location as a crossroads. Through the Gulf of Aqaba in the south, Jordan also has access to the sea. With an area of 37,738 square miles (97,740 square kilometers), Jordan is one of the smaller of the Middle East countries, however, what it lacks in size it makes up with investment opportunities.

Jordan's climate is generally dry. While the western part of the country has a rainy season that lasts from November to April, the wettest parts of the country receiving about 26 inches (66 centimeters) of rainfall annually, the eastern part of the nation approaches desert-like conditions. Temperatures similarly vary with location with the Jordan Valley experiencing extremely hot summer temperatures that may reach 120° F (49° C). Summer temperatures in other parts of the country often average 10 to 20 degrees less than in the valley. Winters are cool with temperatures in some regions occasionally falling below freezing, but there are seldom extended sub-freezing periods.

Jordan has a population of about 4.2 million, of which some 98% are Arab. The country's official language is Arabic, however English is common among the country's professionals and upper classes. English is often the language of choice in Jordan's international business sector. The standard of living in the country is excellent, particularly in Amman, while the telecommunications system throughout the country is of high quality.

Economy and Taxes

In recent years the government of Jordan has undertaken steps to expand the country's economy, which for years has centered around agriculture and a few major industries. Throughout the 1990s these steps have resulted in impressive results, including:

- In 1992, Jordan's GDP grew by 16.1%, which was the highest in the Middle East and North Africa.

- In 1993, Jordan's GDP grew by 5.9% against a regional average of 4.8%.

- In 1994, Jordan's economic growth was 8.1% against a regional average that declined in many locales to 2%.

- In 1995, Jordan's economic growth rate continued to accelerate by 6.4%, which continued to surpass the rates of other nations in the region.

- A growth rate of well over 6% is expected to continue through the year 2,000 and beyond.

- In 1995, exports increased by 24.7% and imports grew by 9.8%.

- Overall, between 1985 and 1995, Jordan's exports grew by 293%.

During the last 20 years, Jordan has emerged as a regional business center, taking advantage of its prime location for trade and commerce. The government has also formulated legislation under the Investment Promotion Law, 1995, which provides for numerous incentives. Under the law foreign investors enjoy the same rights and protections as Jordanian investors in most sectors of the economy, excepting construction contracting, trade services, and mining. The Investment Promotion Law divides the country into three regions – A, B, and C – according to economic indicators. Investors are eligible for specific incentives and exemptions in each region. The amount of tax exemption is determined by the location and type of project, including:

- Projects in Class A Development Regions, 25%.

- Projects in Class B Development Regions, 50%.

- Projects in Class C Development Regions, 7%.

- The projects in the above regions are also entitled to a tax holiday of 10 years.

- Projects planned at one of Amman's industrial areas are eligible to receive an extended "holiday" of two more years.

Contact:

The Jordan Information Bureau
2319 Wyoming Ave., NW
Washington, D.C. 20008
Tel: 202-265-1606
Fax: 202-667-0777

The Embassy of Jordan
3504 International Drive, NW
Washington, D.C. 20008
Tel: 202-966-2664
Fax: 202-966-3110

The Ministry of Industry and Trade
P.O. Box 2019
Amman
Jordan
Tel: 962-6-663191
Fax: 962-6-603721

The Amman Chamber of Commerce
P.O. 287
Amman
Jordan
Tel: 962-6-666151
Fax: 962-6-666155

The Commonwealth of the Northern Mariana Islands

Saipan, Tinia, and Rota are the principal islands of the Northern Marianas, an archipelago of numerous islands located in the western Pacific Ocean. (Guam is also a part of the archipelago, but it is not a member of the Commonwealth.

See the section on Guam, earlier in this chapter.) The overall area of the Marianas is about 184 square miles (477 square kilometers). Saipan is the largest island, with Tinian and Rota next in area. Saipan, home to the islands' government, is a busy seaport and possesses an international airport.

The Marianas enjoy a tropical climate with average annual temperatures of about 83° F (28° C) and little seasonal variation. Sunshine graces most days.

About 45,000 people live on the Marianas, with close to 90% residing on Saipan. The population is comprised of various Pacific people, but also includes Americans, Koreans, Filipinos, Japanese, and Chinese. Several languages are spoken throughout the islands with English, Chamorro (a native language), and Carolinian being official languages. Along with the climate and natural beauty, the excellent standard of living in the Marianas, particularly Saipan, makes the Marianas a true Pacific Paradise.

Economy and Taxes

In an effort to attract investment, the government of the Commonwealth of the Northern Mariana Islands has enacted legislation that provides significant incentives, including:

- A rebate of up to 95% on taxes paid on personal income, provided that such taxes as paid do not surpass $7.5 million. (Residency requirements must be satisfied.)

- A rebate of up to 95% on taxes paid on corporate income, provided that such taxes as paid do not surpass $7.5 million. (Residency requirements must be satisfied.)

- Foreign companies are eligible for federal tax reductions on a part of the income they generate from the sales of exports, provided they conduct their business from a location in the Commonwealth. Moreover, these companies are not required to pay tax to the government of the Commonwealth.

- All ports of entry are free of U.S. Custom duties.

- Specific goods may be exported to the U.S. duty-free and without quota restrictions.

Contact:

Office of the Governor
Administration Building

Capitol Hill
Saipan, MP 96950
Tel: 670-322-5091-92
Fax: 670-322-5096

Marianas Visitors' Authority
P.O. Box 861
Saipan, MP 96950
Tel: 670-664-3200/1
Fax: 670-664-3237

Saipan Division of Revenue and Taxation
Dept. of Finance
CNMI Government
Saipan, MP 96950
Tel: 670-664-1000
Fax: 670-664-1115

Saipan Chamber of Commerce
P.O. Box 806 CHRB
Saipan, MP 96950
Tel: 670-233-7150
Fax: 670-233-7151

Department of Commerce
Commonwealth of the Northern Mariana Islands
Caller Box 10007 CK
Saipan, MP 96950
Tel: 670-664-3000
Fax: 670-664-3066/67

Republic of the Philippines

The Republic of the Philippines is an archipelago consisting of some 7,000 islands, located about 750 miles (1,210 kilometers) east of Vietnam. The total area of the nation is about 115,830 square miles (about 300,000 square kilometers). The islands of the Philippines possess a tropical marine climate with average temperatures ranging between 80° F (27° C) to 94° F (34° C). Most of the islands receive an abundant amount of rainfall.

Of all the islands that comprise the Philippines, 11 – Luzon, Mindanao, Samar, Negros, Palawan, Panay, Mindoro, Leyte, Cebu, Bohol, and Masbate – are the largest and are home to most of the country's population of 75 million people. Malays account for over 90% of the population. With English being one of the country's official languages – Pilipino is the other – the Philippines is the third largest English-speaking nation in the world. The standard of living throughout the islands is good in the major cities but declines in quality in the outlying areas. While the overall infrastructure is adequate, infrastructure, too, is of higher quality in the major cities.

Economy and Taxes

The economy of the Philippines is diversified and focuses on several sectors, including: agriculture, light industry, textiles, chemicals, electronics assembly, pharmaceuticals, wood products, and petroleum refining. In recent years the government has enacted various incentives to promote the nation's economy and particularly its industries. The Omnibus Investment Code, for example, provides incentives to investors who engage in high-priority economic activities, and includes:

- A 100% income tax holiday of six years for pioneer companies and four years for non-pioneer companies. The holiday is extendible for two years.

- An income tax reduction of three years for expansions.

- An exemption from national or local contractor's tax.

- Tax and duty-free importation of capital equipment and spare parts.

- A tax credit on capital equipment obtained from local sources.

- A deduction of labor expenses from taxable income.

Companies that set up operations in "less-developed" areas, as classified by the government, are eligible for special incentives, including:

- A full deduction from taxable income of the costs necessary for infrastructure and public facilities that affects the operation of the company.

- A double-deduction of labor expenses.

The Philippines also has established export processing zones. Companies that establish operations in the zones are eligible for the following incentives:

- An exemption from local taxes.

- An exemption from local licenses and fees.

- An exemption from real estate taxes as applied to production equipment that is not attached to the land.

- A special tax on merchandise within the zone.

- An exemption from the 15% branch profits remittance tax.

Contact:

The Embassy of the Philippines
1600 Massachusetts Ave., NW
Washington, D.C. 20036
Tel: 202-467-9300
Fax: 202-328-7614

The Philippine Department of Tourism
556 Fifth Ave.
New York, NY 10036
Tel: 212-575-7915

The Department of Trade and Industry
Industry and Investment Building
4th Floor
385 Gen. Gil J. Puyat Ave.
Makati City,
Republic of the Philippines
Tel: 632-895-3515
Fax: 632-896-1166

The U.S. Agency for International Development
(USAID)
Ramon Magsaysay Center
1680 Roxas Blvd.
Manila
Philippines
Tel: 632-522-4411
Fax: 632-521-5241

The American Chamber of Commerce of the

Philippines, Inc. (AMCHAM)

2nd Floor, Corinthian Plaza
Paseo de Roxas
Makati City
Philippines
Tel: 632-818-7911 to 15
Fax: 632-816-6359

Seychelles

Seychelles lies in the Indian Ocean, northeast of Madagascar. The country consists of some 118 islands that have an overall area of about 108 square miles (280 square kilometers). The islands possess a tropical marine climate with an average annual temperature of about 75° F (24° C) with little seasonal variation. Rainfall varies among the islands, but in general they all receive generous precipitation.

About 78,000 people live in Seychelles, most of whom have descended from Asians, Africans, and Europeans. English and French are official languages, however, Creole, mostly based on French but including much of the many languages once spoken on the islands, is also common. While the standard of living in the capital, Victoria, is good, the quality of life in some of the outlying areas is not likely to satisfy modern expectations. The infrastructure on the islands is considered to be reliable and among the best of the region.

Economy and Taxes

Seychelles has become a prime tourist site in the Eastern Hemisphere with over 100,000 people visiting the islands annually. Realizing that expansion of the economy depends on more than just tourism, the island government has initiated various programs to attract investment. Seychelles offers numerous tax incentives, including:

- There is no income tax.

- There is no withholding tax on dividends.

- There is no wealth or gift taxes.

- There is no property tax.

- There are no taxes on properties.

- There is no tax on capital gains.

- There are no death duties.

In 1994 the government enacted the Investment Promotion Act to encourage business investment in Seychelles. The Act provides the following incentives:

- A low business tax rate of 15% with further tax credits possible; an effective rate of 9% is possible.

- No import duties on capital equipment.

- Accelerated depreciation schedules of up to 150% of the original cost of assets for certain categories of investments.

- A tax holiday for certain companies.

- Companies that obtain a license under the International Trade Zone Act are exempt from all taxes provided their operations and output are intended for the export market.

- Any changes in taxation after the issue of a Certificate of Approval cannot be detrimental to the company in question.

Seychelles has also positioned itself as a center for the establishment of international trusts. The trust law of Seychelles has many notable features, including:

- The transfer or disposition by an individual who creates an international trust cannot be invalidated by a foreign rule of forced heirship.

- The accumulation of income is not restricted.

- Settlors or trustees can be named as beneficiaries under the trust.

- The settlor chooses the law governing an international trust, and this law is the proper law; the choice may be express or implied in the terms of the trust.

- Confidentiality is maintained. Under the trust law, it is prohibited to disclose or produce any information relating to an international trust, except under an injunction of the Seychelles Supreme Court as a result of an application made by the Seychelles Attorney General. Such applications may be made only in inquiry or trial in relation to the trafficking of narcotics and dangerous drugs, arms trafficking or money laundering.

• There is no requirement to mention the names of the settlor or the name of beneficiary, unless the latter is a Seychellois national or a body corporate resident in Seychelles.

• A one-time registration fee of U.S. $100 is required.

Contact:

Embassy of Seychelles
820 Second Ave.
Suite 900 F
New York, NY 10017
Tel: 212-687-9766
Fax: 212-922-9177

Seychelles Department of Tourism and Transport
Independence House, Victoria
P.O. Box 92
Mahe
Seychelles
Tel: 248-225313, 224030
Fax: 248-224035, 225131

The Republic of Singapore

Singapore is located at the southern tip of the Malay Peninsula. Its position is at the heart of the international trade routes and makes Singapore one of the most important gateways to Asia. Singapore consists of about 50 small islands with a total area of about 224 square miles (580 square kilometers), making the nation smaller than New York City. Singapore is the largest of the islands and home to the capital city, also named Singapore.

Singapore has a tropical climate with an average annual temperature of 81° F (27° C). There is little variation in temperature throughout the year, and although rainfall is relatively consistent, November to January are the wettest months.

About 3 million people live in Singapore with about 77% of the population being Chinese. Malays and Indians make up most of the rest. Because the country is a center of international business, several languages are spoken, the most common being Chinese, Malay, Tamil, and English, which is the language of government and much international business. Singapore's residents and visitors enjoy one of the highest standards of living in Asia. The city of Singapore is considered by many to be among the world's cleanest and safest.

Economy and Taxes

Singapore's diversified economy is one of the strongest of the Far East. Numerous sectors are vital to the economy, including: electronics, pharmaceuticals, chemicals, machinery, plastics, steel, clothing, processed foods, timber products, rubber products, shipbuilding, and oil refining. Global shipping services center around Singapore's deep-water port, which is one of the best and busiest in the region. Financial and business services have gained importance in recent years, making Singapore a trade and finance center.

To promote the economy the government of Singapore has enacted various incentives to encourage investment on the parts of individuals, particularly non-residents, and businesses.

The following tax incentives are aimed at non-resident individuals:

- Non-residents who remain in Singapore for not more than 60 days in a year are not subject to tax.

175

- Non-residents who remain in Singapore for more than 60 days, but less than 183 days in a year, are subject to tax on income from or received in Singapore at a rate applicable to Singapore residents or 15%, whichever is greater.

- Non-residents who remain in Singapore for more than 183 days in a year are considered residents and are taxed at a rate calculated on a sliding scale ranging from 2% on the first $5,000 to 28% on income greater than $400,000.

The following incentives are aimed at businesses. Most business incentives are offered under the Economic Expansion Incentives Act and are administered by the Economic Development Board, the Trade Development Board, the Monetary Authority of Singapore, and the Ministry of Finance. The most important of these incentives, include:

- Manufacturing and high-tech services are eligible for for pioneer tax holidays of up to 10 years. Qualifying enterprises may be eligible for tax reduction for another 10 years.

- Investment allowances of up to 50% are available.

- Financial services enjoy a reduced tax rate.

- Oil traders, international traders, and shippers may qualify for a reduced rate on offshore business.

Contact:

The Singapore Economic Development Board
55 East 59th St.
New York, NY 10022-11122
Tel: 212-421-2200
Fax: 212-421-2206

The Singapore Economic Development Board
180 North Stetson Ave.
Suite 970
Chicago, IL 60601-6712
Tel: 312-565-1100
Fax: 312-565-1994

The Singapore Economic Development Board
1100 New York Ave., NW
Suite 440
Washington, D.C. 20005-1701
Tel: 202-223-2570
Fax: 202-223-2571

The Singapore Economic Development Board
210 Twin Dolphin Dr.
Redwood City, CA 94065-1402
Tel: 650-591-9102
Fax: 650-591-1328

Consulate of the Republic of Singapore
231 East 51st St.
New York, NY 10022
Tel: 212-223-3331
Fax: 212-826-5028

Consulate of the Republic of Singapore
1670 Pine St.
San Francisco, CA 94109
Tel: 415-928-8508
Fax: 415-673-0083

About the Author

Over the past 25 years, Adam Starchild has been the author of over two dozen books, and hundreds of magazine articles, primarily on business and finance. His articles have appeared in a wide range of publications around the world -- including Business Credit, Euromoney, Finance, The Financial Planner, International Living, Offshore Financial Review, Reason, Tax Planning International, The Bull & Bear, Trust & Estates, and many more.

Now semi-retired, he was the president of an international consulting group specializing in banking, finance and the development of new businesses, including tourist enterprises. He has owned and operated travel agencies, travel wholesalers, and tour operators.

Although this formidable testimony to expertise in his field, plus his current preoccupation with other books-in-progress, would not seem to leave time for a well-rounded existence, Starchild has won two Presidential Sports Awards

179

and written several cookbooks, and is currently involved in a number of personal charitable projects.

His personal website is at http://www.adamstarchild.com/

www.ingramcontent.com/pod-product-compliance
Lightning Source LLC
Chambersburg PA
CBHW031933190326
41519CB00007B/519